Table Tennis

For better readability, we have decided to use the masculine (neutral) form of address, but the information also refers to women.

This book has been very carefully prepared, but no responsibility is taken for the correctness of the information it contains. Neither the author nor the publisher can assume liability for any damages or injuries resulting from information contained in this book.

Bernd Ulrich Gross/Werner Schlager

Table Tennis

Tips from a World Champion

Meyer & Meyer Sport

Original title: Tischtennis Perfekt
© 2011 by Meyer & Meyer Verlag
Translated by Regina Stevens

British Library Cataloguing in Publication Data
A catalogue record for this book is available from the British Library

Table Tennis
Tips from a World Champion
Maidenhead: Meyer & Meyer Sport (UK) Ltd., 2011
ISBN 978-1-84126-324-3

© 2011 by Meyer & Meyer Sport (UK) Ltd.
Aachen, Adelaide, Auckland, Budapest, Cape Town, Graz, Indianapolis,
Maidenhead, Olten (CH), Singapore, Toronto
Member of the World
Sport Publishers' Association (WSPA)
www.w-s-p-a.org
Printed by: B.O.S.S Druck und Medien GmbH
ISBN 978-1-84126-324-3
E-Mail: info@m-m-sports.com
www.m-m-sports.com

CONTENTS

PREFACE AND ACKNOWLEDGEMENTS

During my extensive life in the table tennis world I was fortunate enough to attend many wonderful events, and two of them clearly stick out:

In 1989, I was allowed to witness how the young German Double Joerg Rosskopf and Steffen Fetzner sensationally became World Champions in the sold-out Westfalen Halle in Dortmund. The spectators were filled with enthusiasm! Germany experienced a table tennis boom afterward and international table tennis also gained prestige.

The second unforgettable experience happened in 2003 in Paris, where the World Championships took place. Austrian Werner Schlager turned the *Palais Omnisports de Paris-Bercy* into a madhouse. Although Werner was ranked sixth in the world and belonged to the top players, nobody counted on him winning the tournament. The Chinese superiority was thought to be too strong. However, he played better, round after round, as if in trance, close to defeat several times, but he was triumphant in the end. A dream came true, and the 13,000 spectators dreamed with him because they could hardly believe what this Austrian had achieved. Werner has played himself into the hearts of countless table tennis fans, regardless of their nationality.

I am very grateful that I was allowed to watch his last three games. I lived through the games as if I were standing at the table with all his ups and downs. Since Werner was a junior, he had a contract with the Japanese Table Tennis manufacturer *Tamasu Butterfly,* for whom I have been working as a journalist for 20 years. His World Championship title is absolutely brilliant. Before him, Swedish legend Jan-Ove Waldner was the last European to win the World Championships in the men's single.

Werner's title also sparked an enormous table tennis boom in Austria as a result. He is an ambassador for the table tennis sport; he loves his fans and talks to them openly, honestly and without arrogance. He lives table tennis and engages wherever possible. He criticizes developments he sees as going in the wrong direction and has his eye directed toward the future. The foundation of the Werner Schlager Academy in Vienna/Schwechat is the best proof that he will continue to promote table tennis and provide new inspiration.

I want to thank Werner Schlager for his wonderful cooperation during our interviews, which we conducted over a period of two years for the Butterfly Internet Newsletter. He has proven that he is a thoughtful player who reflects upon his sport. He was enthusiastic about my idea to compile these interviews into a book which offers a unique look at the sport.

I would also like to thank (on behalf of Werner, as well) *Tamasu Butterfly Europe* and its director Hideyuki Kamizuru, who supported the idea right from the start and made extensive photographic material available to us.

We wish all the readers much fun and hope you gain new knowledge with this book. May one or another tip help you as a player or coach, for then our work was worth it.

Bernd-Ulrich Gross

1   INTRODUCTION

The basis for this book is a compilation of 23 interviews which I conducted with Werner Schlager throughout 2008 and 2009 for *Butterfly News*. It soon became clear that these interviews would be perfect material for a completely different table tennis instruction book altogether. The interviews were reviewed, brought up to date and summarized. The goal was to produce a clearly structured book in a new form. No table tennis book has offered continuous interviews (apart from the analysis of picture series) until now.

All major aspects of theoretical and practical issues of table tennis are covered. Naturally, the topics about stroke techniques take up most of the space because Werner offers a lot of tips for training and the game, and surely many players and coaches are very interested in this information. Numerous picture series are meant to contribute to a better understanding.

The nice thing about this book is that you do not need to read it in chronological order. The chapters all stand for themselves, so if you are interested in psychology, you can start reading from that section. If you don't know Werner Schlager that well, you should start with his short account of his accomplishments, *A few words from Werner Schlager.* By reading about Werner first, some of the passages in the interviews will be easier to understand.

2 A FEW WORDS FROM WERNER SCHLAGER

The "seatbelt on" sign is off; the plane has landed in Vienna/Schwechat. One week in China is over. Finally, I am at home again.

With my Bettina, and my son Nick.

At home?

Nearly at home. Yes, here in Schwechat it smells like home even if I still live in Vienna Neustadt.

Schwechat – a few minutes from Vienna International Airport, and close to the city itself. In the heart of Europe. There it is – "my" Werner Schlager Academy. A table tennis world training center has been built here in my honor.

A wonderful world is opening: two enormous gyms. In the bigger one, there is table tennis on 30 tables around the clock. A fitness center with all the latest equipment, large rooms for a team of physicians who take care of our guests around the clock, a restaurant, a players lounge, rooms for seminars... everything a top athlete needs.

My world of wonders – our world of wonders.

Werner's start at his father's homemade table

How many fights did I have to win to get all this? How many bridges did I have to cross? What did I have to win?

Win?

Yes – I did win. I did win a lot. It was a long, strenuous path up to the top. A path with a lot of ups and downs.

A path that started more than three decades ago in Vienna Neustadt.

My father Rudolf was fascinated right from the start by his hobby, table tennis. He got it into his head to lead my brother Harald and me to the top. My brother's path ended at the top of Austria. Mine went even farther.

Was I 5 or 6? It doesn't matter – my father had the brilliant idea to saw off the legs of our table tennis table to give me the opportunity to play at a suitable height very early. He made me listen to Polka music so that I could find a playing rhythm.

I don't know how many people laughed at my father at the time, how often they told my father that I would never get anywhere.

They were wrong. Many were wrong.

World Championships in Paris Bercy, a tournament that seemed to be finished for me already the day before. Wang Liquin, the defending champion from China, was leading 3:2 in sets and had 4 match balls at 10:6 in the quarter-final.

I will never get this film out of my head.

Defended.
Defended.
Defended.
Defended.

The moment of triumph:
World Champion 2003!

Thirteen thousand people jumped up and cheered, and I was qualified for the semifinal the next day. And again there was a mountain to climb – the Olympic Champion Kong Linghui – a giant from China. Against him, I had to defend a match ball in the seventh set. A few hours later and six sets against the Korean Joo Se Hyuk and I was standing on the winners' podium listening to the Austrian national anthem. I really had accomplished my win.

I arrived at the Olympic Single World Champion ranked number 1 in the world ranking.

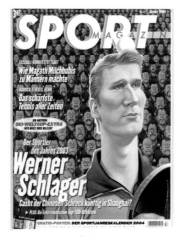

Sportsman of the year in Austria, Idol in China

I couldn't achieve more as a table tennis player. Even then – apart from some setbacks, which accompany every athlete – there are so many hours and days I will never forget.

When I …

… following a poll of the Chinese news agency Xinhua, was the most popular foreign athlete in the world in front of Michael Schumacher, Tiger Woods, Ronaldo, and the tennis player Michael Chang, who was an idol in China his whole life.

…together with my friend Karl Jindrak, won gold in the doubles at the European Championships in Aarhus in 2005.

… among others, sensationally beat my friend Vladimir Samsonov and got to the final at the European Championships in Stuttgart in 2009, where I could not prepare myself properly because I was already busy with the preparations for the Werner Schlager Academy in Schwechat.

Yes, I can talk a lot about three decades.

About my trips around the world, and my experiences in Asia, especially China, where I was always met with a lot of respect.

About the birth of my son Nick, and seeing him grow – a fascinating present from heaven.

About Bettina, the woman of my life, the mother of my son.

And about the Werner Schlager Academy. About the idea, the planning, and the sport political talks, which made the realization of this wonder world possible.

I was so lucky to achieve almost everything an athlete and person can only dream of.

Here and now, I would like to pass on everything I learned as an athlete, a table tennis player and person.

Great coaches stand by my side: "Mister Butterfly" Mario Amizic, who once worked with stars like Vladimir Samsonov, Michael Maze, Petr Korbel, Jun Mizutani and Zoran Primorac.

Richard Prause and Dirk Wagner are on my team – Germany's success coaches, when Timo Boll was rising to number 1 in the world rankings, to the Olympic Final and to a world star.

I found coaches from all over the world, who could help with mental care, physical coaching, advising for nourishment, massage and even physicians – they all should and want to continue with me and my team at the Werner Schlager Academy where I will one day end my career as a player.

"If table tennis would be simple, it would be called football." I read that once on a T-shirt of one of my national team colleagues. Table tennis is not simple – table tennis is a world sport that never rests. It is a sport that develops quickly and will continue to develop quickly. I am not only there with my team, but we are all in the middle of it. One day, we will move forward. It is a long way. I am looking forward to it ...

Werner Schlager
Schwechat, September 2010

A dream comes true: World Champion!

3

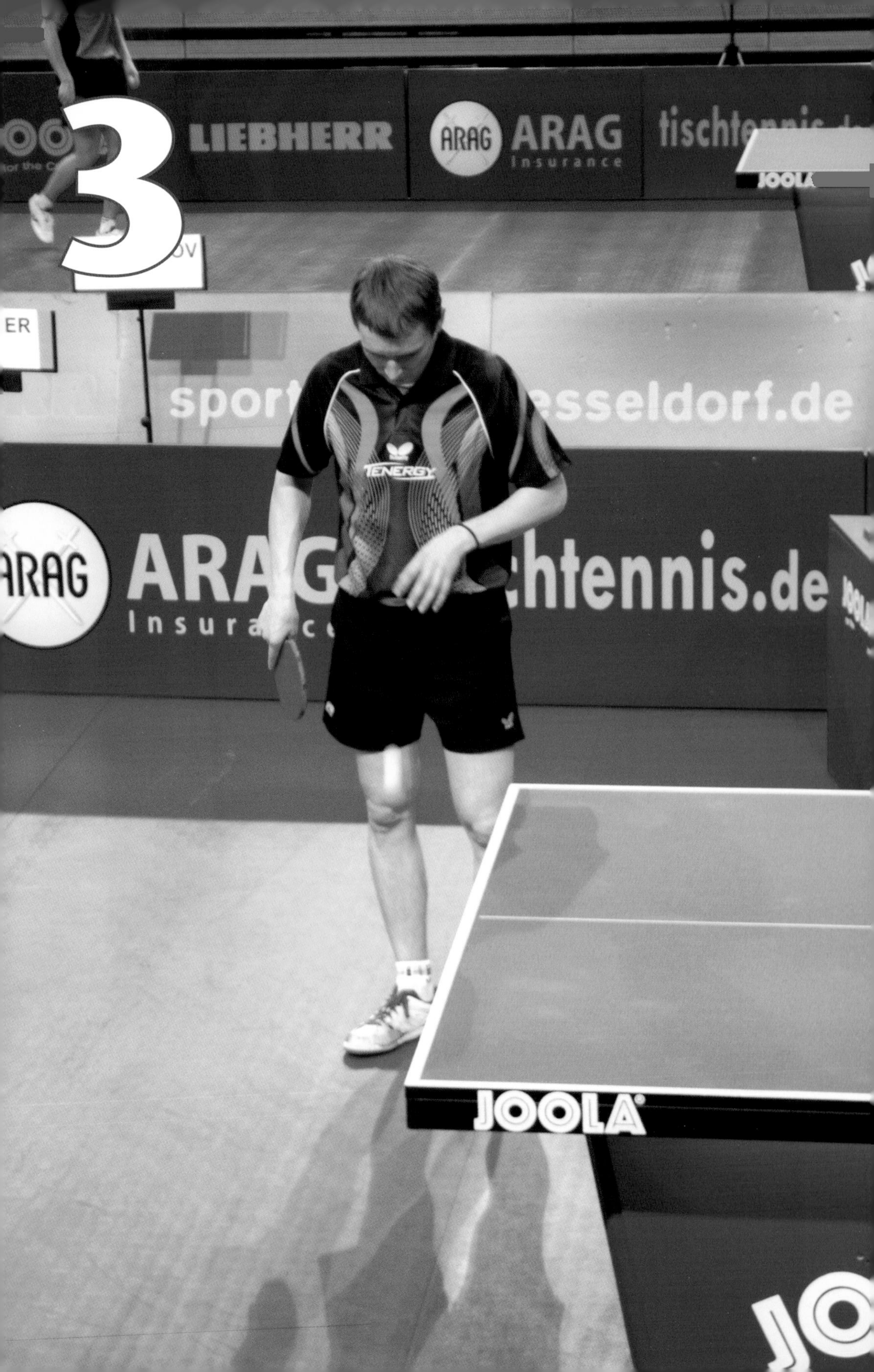

3 ABOUT THE STROKE TECHNIQUES

3.1 The Service

"The service is the most important stroke in table tennis"

The game is opened with a service. It is the only stroke technique that is played without the influence of an opponent. No other technique can be varied so much concerning rotation, placement and speed. It is a stroke technique, which decides the outcome of a game to a large extent. Despite its importance, a lot of amateurs don't pay a lot of attention to service training.

This technique is special. Some love it, some hate it. As the stroke that opens the game, how important is the serve generally?

The service is without a doubt the most important stroke in table tennis. At the same time, it is also the visiting card of each player because the possibilities of variation are endless. A bad serve is very often followed by the loss of a point in the same way a clever and varied serve often leads to winning a point.

There are good servers and not-so-good servers. At the top level, there are surely differences but not as obvious as with amateurs. How important is the serve for your game?

For me, the service is a very important tactical tool.

You prefer serving forehand, but I think I have also seen you serve backhand. What are the advantages of a forehand serve, and when is it worth using the backhand variety?

I practice the forehand serve much more, therefore I use the backhand variety very seldom.

Have you got one secret serve that you keep for important match situations to surprise your opponent?

I have some service varieties that I use very consciously. I would not call it a secret serve though.

There are only a few players, like Samsonov, Primorac, Saive and now Ovtcharov, who frequently serve with their backhand. Is that because of their aptitude, their former coaches or just coincidence?

I would call it preference; a preference that is connected to their aptitude. Not so much in the case of Samsonov (more a tactical variety) than with other players.

Would you tell younger players to practice forehand and backhand serves equally?

Yes, of course. Personal preferences should be supported.

You played in Magdeburg against the young German, Dimitrij Ovtcharov. When I saw him a year ago for the first time, I noticed his unconventional serves straight away. Side spin serves with the forehand from a low position like you saw during the '60s and '70s, and backhand side spin serves that remind me of Stellan Bengtsson or Peter Stellwag. Wang Liqin had big problems with these during the German Open in Bremen. Does this mean that anything is possible with serves?

It shows that serve varieties can be very effective every now and again. The more attention drawn to a special technique, the more it is going to be analyzed and lose its effectiveness. Therefore, all top players must constantly think of new varieties. That is the only way to survive several years as a world class player.

The serve is connected closely to nerves and self-confidence. You have got to be very relaxed and feel loose. Many become too tense when serving and produce direct faults or hand over the advantage to the opponent. Are you familiar with these situations? If so, what can you do to prevent them?

Naturally, I know these situations. I hope that I have learned by now to handle them.

In order to stay relaxed, does it help to shake your forearm every now and again?

Physiologically: yes. Psychologically: no. The basis for each serve, not counting technical ability, is the mental temperament. In my experience, the tension in your hand is rarely a result of too demanding physiological stress on the muscles in your hand.

Which players have the best serves from your point of view at the moment? What is special about them?

Chen Qi or Vladimir Samsonov to name two of many. Naturally, technical ability is very important, but the best servers are also mentally the strongest.

You are playing against an opponent whose serves cause you great problems. What do you do to improve your returns?

I learn from my mistakes.

Have you won matches because of your own good serves?

Yes, there are some players who have had big problems returning my serves. It is only against weak players that this is the only reason for winning a game.

Are there some matches that you lost because of the good serves of your opponent?

Yes, a good serve can be a deciding factor for a game.

Do you think precisely about each serve and which variety you want to use or does it happen automatically?

I always think about which variety I am going to use. The execution should happen automatically.

One of the best servers in the world: Vladimir Samsonov from Belarus

If you look at your service repertoire, how many varieties do you have?

About eight main serves and uncountable varieties.

Some experts maintain that it is better to be in command of fewer service varieties but to execute them perfectly in placement, speed and spin. What do you think about this?

It's all a question of style. Is it better to play a few varieties well or have many varieties that may not be so good? Both are legitimate and successful strategies.

Can you explain to our readers what an "empty" serve is and how you play it?

If you want to play a serve without any spin, you should not put any rotation on it when making contact.

How do you practice the serve? Is it part of every session?

I play competition-related exercises in each session, so services are always included. Sometimes I practice just serves.

Do you always practice serves in combination with a return or do you also take 100 balls out of a box and just hit?

Both ways of training are important.

What is the secret about the Chinese serves? Their serves are not the most spectacular but are very efficient in games. Is their service practice more extensive and of a better quality?

I think that apart from their technical ability, they also achieve above average rotation due to their rubbers ("China rubbers" have a lot of grip), which causes problems for many Europeans.

We could observe a lot of changes in table tennis, especially with the serves, during the past few decades. In which direction is the trend going to go from your point of view?

Everything that hasn't been seen for a while will become a trend again for a short while. That happens automatically. I would like to know myself what is coming next.

When I am serving, *I am very focused.*
When it's 10:10, *I serve as if it is 5:5.*
When I serve an ace, *I am really happy.*
When I miss a serve, *I think:*
"Don't lose your nerve now!"
My serve is *my weapon!*
Service training is *boring but very important.*

Service ritual to increase the concentration

1 = Werner bounces the ball on the floor

2 = puts it briefly in his pocket

3 = goes to the table

4 = bounces the ball on the table

5 = goes down into the deep service position

Services with the Forehand

There are surely topspin players who serve more spectacularly. Werner serves very effectively and dangerously. He also serves traditionally with the same grip, which he uses for playing rallies. This means that he doesn't change his grip for the service to hold the bat between his thumb and index finger. We will only present his forehand serves because he mainly uses those.

The first serve is a forehand backspin serve from the backhand side. The picture series from behind allows a precise view of the speciality of this serve. Afterward, we will compare four variations of this serve concerning their different rotation. At the end, Werner shows us a forehand service where he throws the ball up above his head, which he likes to use in certain situations.

▶ **Picture series 1: Forehand service from the back**

Basic position and backswing: Werner is standing square to the table. One foot is in front of the other. The weight of his bent upper body is on his front leg. Werner is holding the ball right behind the baseline in the palm of his hand just above the table **(1)**. The hand is still down while the upper body is stretching slightly **(2)**. **Picture 3** shows clearly that the upper body is still stretching up. Simultaneously, Werner lifts the back right foot to move it slightly backwards. In picture 4, he stretches the arm with the ball and simultaneously moves the bat backwards and up. At the moment when he releases the ball at the height of his breast, he moves his bodyweight to the back leg **(5, 6)** and lifts the right front leg as seen in **picture 7**. He always keeps his eye on the ball. The peak of the throw up is reached and is about the height of the eyes. Now the stroke movement starts.

Stroke and follow-through: Werner's left leg is raised and the wide open bat is directed towards the falling ball **(8)**. **Picture 9** shows Werner just before making contact with the ball. Considering the position of his body, Werner has pulled up his left leg extremely and puts it down speedily at the moment when he makes contact with the ball. By doing this, the service gets a clear rhythm. In **picture 10,** the ball has just left the bat. Werner has moved his whole bodyweight to the left foot. A comparison of the bat angle in **pictures 9 and 10** indicates a straight backspin or a side-backspin serve. The amount of rotation is not clear. For this, we need to know the speed of the bat at the moment of making contact with the ball. It is also interesting to observe from this perspective how Werner turns his whole body into the serve by rotating the hips. Then Werner follows up the serve and gets into position for the next stroke **(11, 12)**.

▶ Picture series 2: Forehand service variations

In the following four picture series, Werner shows us two basic forms of his forehand service repertoire and four variations. The difference between the two basic forms is the grip. Werner plays variations A and B using the *service grip,* where the fingers let go of the grip and the bat is held between the index finger and the thumb to gain more movement of the wrist. He plays variations C and D with a normal grip because this is better for the services of this category.

The services A and B and C and D differ from the movement of the playing arm and the change of rotation

A: Side spin with a simple stroke direction

When we look at the position of the bat in **pictures A2 and A3,** the amount of spin difference in this classical service variety becomes clear. Everything is possible, from pure side spin or side top spin. Just slight changes of the bat angle and the speed of the bat in this tangential contact with the ball can mean quite a lot of difference in spin. In this case, Werner seems to have hit the ball with a straight bat position so that the ball should have side spin. In this variety, the bat of a right-handed player moves from right to left. The next variation is a bit more complicated.

B: Side spin with a double stroke direction (opposite direction)

This service has two directions of movement because the bat is first taken toward the body and then away from the body. If the ball is hit when the bat is moved toward the body, it has the same rotation as in service variation A. If the ball is hit in the opposite direction, we have a left-right rotation. **Pictures B2 and B3** demonstrate this opposite movement very clearly. The kind of spin depends upon the abovementioned factors. Werner's bat position in **picture B3** hints at side-back spin.

C: Backspin with a horizontal bat position

This service became more popular again after the two variations above became more common. The principle here is that the player hits the ball with a wide open bat angle to gain maximum backspin. Here too the position of the bat is very important and may lead to enormous changes in spin.

29

D: Side-backspin

The difference between variations C and D is that Werner doesn't move the bat forward but moves it to the side of his body. The danger of this service is that the opponent has difficulty seeing when contact with the ball is made: at the moment when the movement of the bat is straight or to the side. Apart from side-backspin, this can also lead to side-topspin.

3.2   Service Return

"The correct reading of a service is a question of experience in competition and training."

The return of the service is not one particular technique but a whole series of stroke techniques that are suitable to answer a serve. Short services, depending on their rotation and height, are returned with a long or short push or a flip, whereas long serves are looped with a lot of different topspin varieties. The key to returning a service well is to anticipate the service early (concerning the placement and rotation) so that you can use the right technique for the return. Almost equally important is the return of the serve.

The service return is not one particular technique but a whole series of strokes that can be used to play back the ball. What determines a good return?

A good return can force the server into a passive role.

Looking at your returns, where are your strengths and weaknesses?

My strength is variety, my weakness is the varying quality of the returns.

The advantages of the server against the returning player might be great at lower levels but among top players, it can't be as great. Two different research studies show that the advantages for the server were 53% to 47% or 51% to 49%. Another study even showed an advantage of 51% to 49% for the returning player. If you compare your serves with your returns, where do you think you are stronger?

Werner in the return position from two perspectives

I think the majority of players consider serving as an advantage. It would be interesting to find out if that is true. I also think that my serves are better than my returns, although I sometimes feel differently during matches.

What characterizes a good return player?

Some players can anticipate serves very well, others react better and others have a good awareness of the ball's action.

One of the main conditions for an optimal return is the early judgement about the coming serve, concerning rotation, placement and speed. In this context, we talk about being able to read the serve, which is exactly what many young inexperienced players are lacking. How can you learn to do this and improve it?

Start of the match: Both players, the Croatian Zoran Primorac serving, Werner Schlager returning, take up their positions

Only through a lot of competition experience. Every player has his own technique and tactics when serving. The possibilities of variations are endless.

Experience plays an important role when reading a serve. Do you have an advantage returning the serve when you have played more often against a player?

Yes, of course. The more often you have played against a player, the better you should be able to return the serve.

Are there top players whose serves (despite intensive analysis) still cause you problems?

Yes, there are some players whose serves I simply can't read. I don't want to say who they are. Either the quality of the serves is extremely high or the variation takes me by surprise again and again.

In which way does a bad return influence your self-confidence? Often players lose their head when they can't return the serves. How can you still try to stay in the game?

A bad return increases the pressure to win the point when you are serving. Many players can't manage the extra pressure. You should try to concentrate on your strengths, not your weaknesses.

When watching top players, you can see that they perform certain rituals before they take up their returning position to achieve the highest possible concentration level. What do you do?

I am not aware of any rituals. I mainly concentrate on my breathing to slow down my pulse rate.

Some players bend down a lot for their returning position (e.g., Boll) others do this less (e.g., Ma Lin or Wang Liqin). Some are close to the table, some farther away. Which position would you recommend?

I don't like extremes, but basically anything is allowed. Everybody should find their own positions and suitable tension.

The position depends upon the opponent and changes accordingly from the far backhand side to the middle of the table with offensive players. What is your position against right-handed and left-handed players? Are there other factors for changing the returning position?

Against players different from yourself, you should move to the middle to be able to read the service better. It is also important whether you return with your forehand or backhand.

How can you improve your return apart from reading the ball?

Only by experience, which means training.

There are still players at the lower levels trying to hide their forehand serves. There are no neutral umpires so there are often arguments. You are known as a very fair player. Are there still players among the professionals who come close to the limit and how do you deal with it?

Of course there are still players who behave unfairly. According to my personal estimation of my opponent's intentions, I react differently. It is a pity that sometimes enthusiasm defeats fairness. Everybody with a little bit of experience should know though that nature pays things back, an eye for an eye.

When I must return the ball,
I must be prepared for anything.
If I don't return two serves in a row,
I get angry.
Before I take up my returning position,
I breathe deeply.
If the serve of my opponent is hidden,
I complain.
Long serves are
often dangerous.
Without short serves,
you can't manage.

3.3   Push

"The push is underestimated in its effect."

The push is one of the basic techniques in which you can place the ball with more or less backspin on the whole table. It is not a spectacular stroke, but it demands a lot of awareness. Played short (for example, as a return to a short backspin service), the push should prevent the opponent from attacking. A long aggressive push with a lot of backspin should lead the opponent to make a mistake. It is part of the basic repertoire of every top player and should always be trained intensively. This is often neglected at the amateur level because the push is not as attractive as the topspin.

How important is the push nowadays at the top level?

Very important because 80% of the rallies include at least one push.

In which game situations?

Mainly with one of the first balls following the service.

Are you practicing the push?

Of course, in every exercise that is competition related.

What are the varieties and in which situations?

The classic push is the short placed push. The other variety is the aggressive-fast and long push. Additionally there are numerous other and less important varieties with sidespin.

Did you have to push a lot in training as a young player?

Yes, in the past there was a lot more pushing in the training sessions.

For many coaches at junior level, the push is not so important any more. Is this right or wrong (of them to not emphasize it)?

Werner returns a short service of the Croatian Zoran Primorac with a backhand push

Wrong. I can't believe that many coaches think like that.

What is more difficult: a backhand or a forehand push? Are there some special tips?

The forehand is more difficult because in a certain area in front of the body, the shoulder joint is not made for a push. Tip: It is better to push a ball in the middle of the body with your backhand.

Does a fast bat (thick sponge and fast blade) make pushing more difficult?

Definitely. The more sensitive a rubber is in regards to rotation, the more exact the bat angle has to be. The faster a bat or rubber is, the more control and awareness you need when you hit the ball. The consistency of a push suffers from a fast bat-rubber combination, and it is only possible to achieve this fine awareness for a push by a lot of training.

How can you improve the use of the wrist, so-called "hacking?" Also, do you know a better term for that?

I think the use of the wrist when pushing is an advantage but not absolutely necessary. The fast movement of the forearm is at least equally important. You must practice a lot if you want to improve the consistency and quality of a push.

You talked above about an aggressive and long variety of a push, which is mainly used against short balls and may often lead to a straight point if it is played well. This push, which can be played with the backhand as well as the forehand, demands a lot of awareness and technique. How important is this push variety?

The better you become, the more important it is to have many technical possibilities. There is no top 100 player in the world who does not use the aggressive long push with the forehand.

The most dangerous element with the push is the change in spin that means to push with a lot, medium or no backspin. What is important here?

The less spin I want to put on the ball, the better I must estimate the spin on the ball and vice versa: The less I know about how much spin is on the ball, the more spin I should use.

What are the biggest mistakes you can make with the push?

You should try to hit the ball as soon as possible after the bounce, and you should push with different varieties.

Do you know exercises juniors can use to improve the push?

Exercises where you push a lot. The best are exercises that are competition orientated and include a service.

Is it true that the Chinese are best in pushing?

Probably. Their rubbers have a lot of grip, which forces them to practice the push more.

If you have a good saying about the push, let us know. My first junior coach always said: If you can't push, you can't play table tennis.

He was definitely right, only because a push is not known for being spectacular, although that can be the case. It is underestimated in its effect.

The push is *elementary* for new beginners.
The push is *underestimated* in top table tennis.
To push consistently *is the most important thing.*
I practice pushing *daily.*
If you can't push, *you must have a good flip.*

Picture series 6 starting on page 70 shows Werner with a short push return

3.4   Drive

"The drive gives me control over my strokes, my movement and my rhythm."

Just like the push, the drive is one of the basic strokes. There is less forward rotation with a drive than with the topspin. Because the ball is hit more centrally, the ball is hit more than brushed. With beginners, it is often one of the first techniques introduced. Nowadays, the drive has a less important role in table tennis at the top level. The time of the drive players in the men's category is long gone and among the women, there are only a few. Yet, the drive is still included in every training session and as a warm-up at the table.

When you talk about the drive, every player in a club thinks automatically about a warm-up with the forehand and backhand. Is it a useful ritual or a stupid habit?

It is a useful ritual.

Do you also use the drive as a warm-up or do you start straight with the topspin?

I usually start with the drive and then the topspin. I get good control over my strokes, movement and rhythm.

The drive is known as an offensive basic stroke. Thirty years ago, it was still used successfully at the top level. The legendary English top player, Desmond Douglas, was a "drive machine." Does the drive in spin-orientated table tennis still have an important meaning today? In which game situation is it used?

In the men's competition, it is only used as an emergency stroke. From my point of view, the reason for that is that the topspin is a safer stroke through the rotation on the ball. I need to know the exact rotation of the ball if I want to play a safe drive with the rubbers we have today. Therefore, the classical drive players, such as Johnny Huang or all the classical "penholder" Asians like Liu Guoliang, Toshio Tasaki, He Zhi Wen, play with short pimples.

Some books say that the drive is a speed reduced smash. What do you think about that?

Correct. According to that, the drive players today should be called "hit players."

The drive is ideal to practice fast rhythm: footwork with shifting the weight of the legs, body and stroke arm coordination, reaction and timing. Do you agree?

Yes, absolutely.

The wrist should be fixed when you play the forehand drive, whereas the wrist plays an important role with the backhand drive. Do you agree and can you explain to our readers the exact role of the wrist for a backhand drive?

Just for the drive, you don't need the wrist. But if the drive is turned into a smash, I have this solution: The movement of the hand is shorter with the backhand drive and the necessary power is missing for a faster stroke. This power is gained by additional wrist movement. The disadvantage lies in additional mistakes (that originate) from the wrist. Therefore, you should not use it for a forehand drive.

Do you have some advice for how to easier learn the backhand drive? The forehand drive is usually easier for new beginners.

The fast drive or the drive with the use of the wrist demands a lot of training. Therefore, you should be satisfied with a backhand drive without using the wrist at the beginning.

At the junior level, the so-called **control exercises** *are often counted 10x, 20x, 30x and so on over the net without a mistake. This is supposed to increase stroke consistency and concentration. What do you think about such control exercises?*

This is the right way to achieve more consistency (and not only for the drive).

Could you explain the exact difference between a forehand topspin and a forehand drive? From the outside, you hardly notice a difference between the short forehand or backhand movements, for example a counter topspin above the table.

For me, the topspin is defined by the spin I put on the ball. With the drive, I just leave the existing spin.

In the lower classes, you can still find the typical drive players who seek a fast game starting with a long serve. They often play with short pimples on the backhand. Is it easier to play the drive with those?

Yes, as I said above, it is easier to play the drive with rubbers that don't have so much grip.

Did you practice the drive a lot when you were young?

I can't remember a lot of drive exercises. I think I moved on to the topspin very soon, at least with my forehand. I developed my backhand topspin later.

Are there still exercises for you where the drive plays an important role?

No, I only practice the drive during the warm-up.

The drive is *quite unimportant* in top table tennis.
The classical drive player is *usually a female.*
The drive is *an important stroke* for the new beginner.
50 times forehand-forehand drive is
a good exercise for new beginners.
A warm-up without the drive *may increase the probability of an injury.*
The backhand drive is, *every now and again, a good surprise*
in comparison to the forehand drive.

3.5   Smash

"The smash is safest at peak bounce"

The smash is related to the drive against low or half-high balls. The speed of the bat and the use of the body are at a maximum and the movement of the playing arm is clearly longer. Against high balls, the top players sometimes use a jump technique. The ball is always hit centrally. As a spectacular final stroke, it is supposed to lead directly to winning the point.

It doesn't matter if you are a hobby or club player, but to master a smash is considered an art. "Wow, he has got a hard smash!" is an exclamation that you may often hear and explains the admiration of this technique. What is so fascinating about the smash?

Obviously, the brutality, which gives the smash speed. The speed again is one reason for its effectiveness.

The topspin has also taken over from the smash as a so-called point winning final stroke in modern offensive table tennis. And still, the smash with the backhand, as well as the forehand, is part of the basic repertoire of every top player. In which game situations do you still use the smash?

In situations where I don't have time to play a topspin. It is an emergency stroke. I also use it in the classical way as an answer to very high and/or short balls.

The ball is hit centrally when smashing. So it doesn't get any forward rotation in comparison to the topspin. Are smashes therefore more risky than topspin balls?

Werner's extreme use of the playing arm for a backhand smash

Definitely. The lack of stabilizing rotation has less consistency as a result.

What is a so-called "smash spin," a mixture of the topspin and a smash? Or is this technique just a crazy idea of clever table tennis people?

No, quite the opposite. Practically, you get a reasonable mixture of effectiveness (speed) and consistency (rotation).

The backhand smash is often compared to a whip. Is that a hint toward the extreme use of the wrist when smashing with the backhand?

Well, possibly. But the more you use the wrist, the more difficult consistency becomes.

When do you play a backhand smash, which (in comparison to the forehand smash) is less important?

I use it only when the ball is played unusually high and/or short to my backhand.

Most books say that the forehand smash is played without the use of the wrist. How do you smash with your forehand?

The shorter the ball is, the more I use my wrist just to be on the safe side.

When you play against backspin defence (for example, as you did in the famous World Championships final 2003 against the Korean Joo Se Hyuk) when do you decide to use a smash?

I decide to smash if the ball is short and/or high enough.

A game situation, which always fascinates table tennis fans, is the smash against the balloon defence. There you can see different timing of when the ball is smashed. Mainly, the ball is hit at peak bounce but sometimes also very early or when it is falling down. Where is the optimal point of making contact with the ball?

The moment of contact is always dependent upon an evaluation of effectiveness and consistency. The earlier I take the ball, the more effective it is but the risk is higher. It is safest to play the ball at peak bounce. You should not take it later because it is less effective and less consistent. In my experience, it is also depends upon the preference of the individual player.

Table tennis demands extreme body application: Kalinikos Kreanga jumping up for a forehand smash

The forehand smash, especially against balloon balls, is often described as the most athletic one. Many topspin players (including you) show jump strokes similar to the javelin throw where the jump technique is combined with the stroke. What is difficult about a forehand smash?

The whole body is involved in the stroke, which makes the coordination of the stroke difficult. The jump makes it even more difficult, which should be avoided. The jump technique is only used to hit the ball at peak bounce against balloon defence. The jump stroke is very attractive but, from my point of view, an emergency stroke.

Do you like the game situation balloon defence smash? With some players, I get the impression that they are glad to hit against the balloon player, others seem more anxious to miss the ball.

I am always happy about the possibility to smash. Some players though have little experience with smashing. Fear is probably written right on their faces.

Smashing a high ball is often compared to a penalty in football. If you miss a seemingly simple high ball, you miss a penalty. It is an annoying ball and hard to swallow. Often such penalties turn a whole match around. Did you experience that yourself or could you observe that in another important match?

Naturally, I missed some penalties or watched colleagues do it. But you should not get insecure because of that.

How do you deal with a missed penalty?

Not differently than with any other mistake. Short analysis; take in the solution, finish.

Which technical-tactical mistakes are often seen with a smash?

Impatience.

Is there one player with the hardest smash, and what is special about it?

The South Korean Oh Sang Eun has the best smash in my opinion. It is very effective and consistent.

The smash is often neglected at amateur level, sometimes even forgotten. How and how often do you train the smash? Are there special exercises?

There are always smashes in training matches. Thanks to my experience, I don't need extra training for that.

If you can smash, *you have a clear advantage.*
If you miss a smash, *you are absolutely surprised.*
If you don't enjoy smashing, *you don't enjoy anything.*
If you play a brilliant smash, *it makes you very happy.*

3.6   Forehand Topspin

"A good topspin player needs the right mix of consistency, precision and speed."

The central stroke in modern offensive table tennis is the topspin, not only in Europe but also in China and the other Asian table tennis nations. With the topspin, the ball is hit tangentially. The ball has a bent flight path and becomes shorter. The topspin can be played against backspin and topspin balls. That way the topspin is an all-around weapon that can be varied a lot concerning speed and spin. Today, the topspin has taken over from the smash as a final point-winning stroke. In this interview, the forehand topspin is the main focus of the questions and the backhand topspin will follow.

What is the advantage of a topspin game in comparison to the classical smash attack with attacking pimples?

With the topspin, you put a lot of forward rotation on the ball and it gets a more stable flight path. The more topspin I put on the ball, the less I need to consider the existing rotation of the coming ball. The advantage is a lot more consistency.

How high is the percentage of a forehand topspin in your attacking game?

Timo Boll, the number one in Europe, with a short arm movement for a forehand top-spin ... the Greek topspin specialist Kalinikos Kreanga with a long movement

I guess about two thirds.

Today, every top player must be in command of a backhand topspin, too. In which situations do you decide to move around to the backhand side to play a forehand topspin?

Only if it makes sense from a tactical point of view, and if I have enough time to move around.

The books about table tennis differentiate between the topspin against topspin and against backspin. What is the difference and which is more difficult?

The difference lies mainly in the angle of the bat, which you must vary according to the rotation of the ball. Personally, I don't see a clear difference between the topspin against topspin or backspin. The transition is fluent if you consider the main factors like main stroke direction and use of the body (more upwards or forwards). The more backspin a coming ball has, the more physically exhausting it is to loop the ball over the net. Technically, the topspin against topspin and backspin are equally difficult.

How important is the use of the wrist with the forehand topspin? The Chinese seem to use it a lot, the Europeans less. Is the material important too?

The use of the wrist plays, just like all the other factors that influence rotation, a role. The same applies to the material. The typical penholder player needs a movable wrist, which he is obviously using more. I doubt that the Chinese shakehand players use their wrists more than we do.

I can remember well my first tries of a topspin. I only learned it properly when I played regularly against defenders. Can you also remember this experience?

Yes, for me it was the first backhand counter topspin. I was practicing with my brother and standing a little bit farther away from the table. My brother was playing topspins to my backhand. Although I was in the passive role, I suddenly decided to loop against it. That was pure intuition. After I recognized what I had done, I was really happy about it, even more than I was when I saw the surprised facial expression of my older brother.

What is the making of a good topspin player? The speed of the spin is surely only one of the factors, but in the lower classes sadly enough dominate because young players only want to loop as fast as possible.

It is the right mix of consistency, precision and speed.

How do you improve consistency and control of your topspin?

By training, training, training.

The forehand topspin is executed quite differently at top level. There are players like Wang Liqin, Ma Lin or Kalinikos Kreanga, who play the topspin with a nearly outstretched arm or others like Timo Boll or Michael Maze, who play with their arm bent and an explosive acceleration of the forearm. Which group do you belong to?

The first group.

What is the secret of a forehand topspin, the control of the ball, the wrist, the acceleration of the arm, the use of the body...?

The right combination of everything.

When playing topspin against topspin, we differentiate between situations "close to/above the table and away/ half-distance." What is important when we loop close to/above the table and what is important when playing from half-distance?

Mainly it is important to estimate the existing rotation and the speed of the coming ball correctly, especially when you are close to the table, because the ball must be hit with a lot of control otherwise it will go out. That way you force your will onto the ball, which means the existing rotation is deciding the following flight path. The farther away from the table you are, the more powerfully you can play the ball. The existing rotation is not as important in comparison to what I want to do.

What kind of topspin variety is the forehand sidespin exactly, which effect does it have, and in which situations is it played?

The sidespin is one of the numerous varieties of the topspin. Its effect is a horizontally bent ("Banana Topspin") flight path, as well as a "side kick" when taking off. It can be used at any time to disturb the rhythm of the opponent.

Who are the best topspin players at the moment and why?

One of the best topspin players is Kalinikos Kreanga. One who uses most varieties is Vladimir Samsonov. One who plays the fastest forehand is Ma Lin. There are a few more who deserve to be named. At the world top level, everybody must be able to play a forehand topspin perfectly and with variety.

Many maintain that new beginners should start with thin rubbers (1,5-1,7mm) because you have better control and more feeling for the ball. Others say it would be very advisable for talented new beginners to play with thick (1,9-2,1mm) rubbers as soon as possible. What is your opinion?

Play with thick rubbers right from the start. A change of bat – rubber, thickness, blade – demands a complete adjustment of movements. You should ask a player to do this as little as possible.

When you think about your own forehand topspin game, what can you still improve on?

A lot, especially consistency.

The forehand topspin surely plays an important role in your training. Can you tell us about one exercise that is very important for you, which you enjoy and often repeat?

My standard exercise is "1-1". It works like this: one backhand from the backhand side, one forehand from the forehand side toward the backhand of my partner. At the beginning I do this regularly, then irregularly and free. If you use different varieties, it is a perfect exercise to improve topspin consistency.

You don't get far at the top level without a forehand topspin.
A good forehand topspin player *has the nose in front.*
If I think about my forehand topspin,
I think about shifting weight optimally.
You need *fast legs* for a forehand topspin.
If I miss a forehand topspin, *my legs were often too slow.*
Footwork *is everything* for a forehand topspin.

▶ **Picture series 3: Werner Schlager's Forehand Topspin at the Table**

In this picture series, Werner shows us one of his dreaded forehand topspins. He can play this stroke in all game situations and with a lot of variety. In this case, he is showing us one forehand topspin variation, which he is playing close to the table, almost only using his arm and his feet parallel. This is "economical" because the little movement of this short forehand topspin has the advantage that it can be executed effectively despite the time pressure of the opponent's attack. It can be used, for example, as a counter topspin against a topspin of the opponent or as an aggressive answer to a flip or an offensive push from the opponent. A player can become more active or change a passive starting position in an active one as a surprise.

Let's now have a look at Werner Schlager's forehand topspin at the table. We can look at the movement from the side **(1-6)**, from the back **(A-C)** and from the front **(D-F)**. Everything is about the same sequence of movement.

Preparation: Werner is standing in the starting position for a following forehand topspin **(1+A)**. The position of his feet is parallel, more than shoulder width apart and slightly square to the table. He is just starting the backswing because he takes his playing arm backwards and down **(2+B)**. In these **pictures (3+C+D)**,

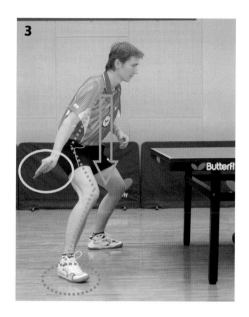

Werner takes his bat into the optimal backswing position for the following stroke. The start of the stroke is slightly below the table. For a topspin against backspin, the backswing of the player must be lower. Altogether Werner has lowered the main weight of his body by bending his knees and hips, a look at the feet shows that he has kept his basic position from **picture 1**. At the end of the backswing, his playing arm is almost fully stretched. This becomes clear in the view from the back **(D).** This picture also shows quite clearly how Werner has lowered his main bodyweight by bending his knees and in the distance between his feet.

Stroke and follow-through: Picture 4 shows Werner after he has made contact with the ball, picture E may be exactly at the moment when he is making contact. Both pictures prove that

- Werner has his playing arm almost fully stretched and the bat is angled backwards and down at the moment of making contact with the ball
- he hits the ball very early (Picture 4), perhaps even above the table **(Picture B)**
- he shifts his bodyweight from the right to the left leg during the stroke (compare **D, E, F**)
- the upper body rotates during the stroke for support (compare **D with F and 3 with 5**).

The bat is closed and the path of the stroke is a straight line forward and up.

The following follow-through shows that Werner's counter topspin from the side **(Pictures 5/6)** or from the back **(Picture G)** look slightly different and are not exactly the same stroke. In pictures 5/6, Werner's backswing is very short. In **picture 6**, he takes his bat back to the basic position. A comparison of **picture 3** and **picture 5** shows how short the stroke of this topspin variety is. This also becomes clear in the view from behind. This stroke seems to be a lot harder than the one from the side considering the intensity because the follow-through ends up beside his head.

55

▶ Picture series 4: Stroke Combination: Forehand Topspin-Backhand Topspin from the Backhand Side

Here Werner shows us an active return of a service with a forehand topspin with a lot of control and spin. He reacts to the opponent's return with a powerful backhand topspin.

Werner is standing in the typical neutral position on the backhand side expecting the service (1). He is standing slightly square to the table. After he has anticipated the service of his opponent, he jumps around the backhand side (2-4) and prepares for a forehand topspin (5). At the end of the backswing (6), he is beside the table and his upper body is opened toward the ball. His stroke movement is directed straight upward. **Picture 7** shows the contact with the ball. The ball is hidden by the bat. At the end of the follow-through, he has shifted his weight toward the front left leg (8, 9)

to take over the bodyweight. The bat is at the height of his head. In **pictures 10, 11, 12,** he jumps away from the table to prepare for the backswing of a backhand topspin **(13).** At the end of the backswing **(14),** the elbow and shoulder of the playing arm are in front again and a very powerful and fast backhand topspin follows **(15).** The stroke direction is forward and up and the bat is closed, which indicates a counter topspin.

3.7   Backhand Topspin

"The backhand topspin is not particularly difficult to learn"

The backhand topspin was developed later than the forehand topspin. Even in the '80s there were top class players without a backhand topspin. Players moved around to the backhand side much more. That has changed completely over the past twenty years. A top player without a backhand topspin doesn't exist anymore. The speed of the game has increased so drastically that it is not possible to move with your forehand to your backhand side permanently. When the Chinese were running after the Europeans in the mid '90s, the pressure was on and they developed a new stroke technique for their penholder players: the backhand topspin for penholders. The reigning World Champion Wang Hao is not the only one who plays it perfectly, but so do all his other penholder colleagues.

The central stroke technique in modern offensive table tennis is surely the forehand topspin, but without a backhand topspin, no offensive player in the world can exist any longer. Or do you know of one?

The representatives of the classic penholder system don't play a proper backhand topspin. The Korean Ryu Seung Min even became Olympic Champion 2004 in Athens with his style. With incredibly fast legs, a back, elastic-like rubber and brilliant anticipation. You can also get to the top without a backhand topspin.

But the top Chinese with a penholder grip can now play a penholder backhand topspin, which can't be compared to the shake-hand backhand topspin but is still very dangerous. Which Chinese has the most dangerous penholder backhand topspin?

From my point of view, it is Wang Hao.

In Europe, the backhand topspin was invented, or let's say developed, during the '70s. It was mainly the Hungarians Tibor Klampar and Gabor Gergely, then the Swedes with Jan-Ove Waldner ahead of everybody and then there were many, many more. Today, everybody must be in command of a backhand topspin. Who are the best backhand topspin specialists to you?

I immediately think of Kreanga, Samsonov and Korbl. I think I too play a sweet backhand topspin.

When did you learn the backhand topspin? Did you have an idol?

I can't remember when exactly I learned it. It must have been during my first years as a cadet. Later, my idol was Tibor Klampar. He played a backhand topspin very close to the table and made life difficult for his opponents.

How important is the backhand topspin for your game?

Very important, because it is often my first active stroke.

Why is it necessary for an offensive player to be able to play a backhand topspin today and in which situations?

Jan-Ove Waldner, the Swedish table tennis genius, with a perfect backhand topspin game

If you want to put the opponent under pressure, you must be able to play safe, good and fast balls from both sides. Even against defenders, a good backhand topspin is a good interruption or you need to have the physical talents of a Ryu Seung Min.

Generally, the backhand topspin is known as a difficult technique for kids to learn. Is that true?

I don't think that it is particularly difficult. The coaches probably spend more attention on the forehand topspin. If their player misses with the forehand or is too slow with his legs then he must compensate with a good backhand. I think it is first of all down to the coaches and the physical condition of the children.

The use of the wrist and the acceleration of the forearm play a major role with the backhand topspin. It is often helpful for children learning a movement to compare it to similar movements they know. The backhand topspin is often associated with throwing a Frisbee. Do you agree or do you have better advice?

The Chinese Single World Champion of 2009, Wang Hao, with a penholder backhand topspin

It is a good comparison for new beginners. But, as with many techniques, only a lot of training really helps.

If we compare your backhand topspin to Timo Boll or Kalin Kreanga, where are the differences?

I think Timo and I play with a similar short backhand movement, most of the time close to the table and rarely far away from the table. Kreanga is a champion of the topspin far away from the table.

The backhand topspin is played like the forehand topspin at different times when you make contact with the ball – above the table, close to the table or from half-distance. Which place of contact is the most difficult?

I think that they are all equally difficult or easy. It is only a question of which varieties you practice most intensively.

In the final of the World Championships 2003, you played against the South Korean defence artist Joo Se Hyuk. It was a legendary match, and you won. It was noticeable though that you hardly used backhand spins but mainly forehand. Was it tactic, a question of time or the fact that your forehand is more powerful against backspin?

The forehand topspin is used more often and therefore is also the most consistent. Therefore, it is the first choice against defence. Somebody who also has a good backhand topspin can use it, of course. It is a good tactic to disturb the flow of the game. The backhand topspin gives the ball a different rotation, a different flight path and a different depth of stroke. The defender must think differently.

At the amateur level, you can observe players who practice one to three times a week and see that they are vulnerable on the backhand side especially with the backhand topspin. "I don't get one backhand on the table," or "My backhand spin is completely off," are comments you hear quite often. Does psychological stress have greater consequences for the backhand because you need finer movements? Did it happen to you and what can you do against it?

Naturally, I had the same experience. Everybody has had it. In my opinion, the feeling of insecurity is based on a lack of training. It doesn't matter which stroke it is. In training, you should work on the experiences from the competition and work on the deficits.

The abovementioned group of players also has the problem that they don't use the backhand topspin correctly in their game from a tactical point of view but use it just as they please and according to the form on the day. If everything goes well, he plays everything with his backhand; if it is going badly, he only plays forehand. Could you give some advice to these players?

Here, only the standard tip is useful: training, training and training.

You said in your comments about the forehand topspin that the backhand topspin is about 30% of your attacking game. In which situations do you use it most?

When the game situation demands it. That means, when an attacking ball is successful, but I don't have time to move around to the backhand side or it doesn't make any sense.

Is there an exercise you prefer to practice the backhand topspin?

That is an exercise for competition where the return is a long ball with backspin to my backhand and I must start with a backhand.

How thick should the sponge of an offensive rubber be to play a good backhand topspin?

The more aggressively you define your offensive stroke, the thicker the sponge should be.

My backhand topspin *is my strength.*
I play a backhand topspin *when it is possible.*
New beginners should *learn* a backhand topspin
after they can do all the basic strokes.
If you play against a player with a good backhand topspin,
play to his forehand.
It is completely normal for me to win a point with my backhand topspin.

Picture series 5: Backhand Topspin

Werner is a backhand specialist. It becomes obvious when we look at game situations where he returns a service, which is placed to his forehand side, with his backhand. Accordingly, his backhand topspin game has a lot of varieties and is very dangerous. The following picture series shows Werner executing a basic backhand topspin.

Preparation and backswing: In the starting position **(1)** Werner is standing in an optimal basic position:
- His legs are parallel, more than shoulder-width apart.
- The knees are slightly bent, which lowers the main bodyweight and creates tension in the muscles of the leg.
- The upper body is slightly bent forward so that the bodyweight is more on the front feet.
- The bat is in the so-called neutral position, which means in the middle of the body.

- As Werner is going to play the ball diagonally, his stance is a bit open to the forehand side

These five movement features enable Werner, in expectation of the coming ball, to move more easily, react quicker and provide him with more choices for the following stroke technique.

Werner is now preparing for his stroke **(2)** by lowering the upper body forward and taking the bat backwards and down.

Werner is reaching the lowest point of his backswing **(3)**. His body is now above the ball and the right shoulder of his playing arm is turned forward a bit. The elbow of the playing arm is in front of the bat, which causes optimal tension in the muscles of the upper arm. The ideal tension in the muscles of the lower arm is achieved by the extreme use of the wrist. Werner takes the bat backwards and down, as if he is going to throw a Frisbee. This pre-tension is absolutely necessary to achieve a lot of speed with the bat during the stroke. It is also important that the bat is almost in-between the legs and not at the side of the body as you can see it occasionally. The player is getting absolute control of the stroke.

Stroke and follow-through: Ideally, Werner hits the ball in front of his body roughly at the height of his stomach **(4)**. The movement of the stroke is a straight line from square down to forward and upward. The bat is closed and brushes the ball to apply as much rotation as possible. The picture seems to be taken a few millimeters before he makes contact with the ball because the head of the bat is still sideways and back. The wrist, which is bent backwards, can be seen clearly. By looking at picture 5, you can guess what is going to happen in the next split second, because the wrist must speedily go upward and forward at the moment of contact with the ball. Only then can the stroke be successful. This is also the reason why the backhand topspin is technically a very demanding stroke, and where the player needs optimal timing and fine coordination. The players who have got the so-called *"hand"* are normally those who have a very good control over the ball and use their wrist brilliantly.

The end of the follow-through **(5)** is reached. The wrist is in the basic position, the head of the bat points forward and up, and the arm is almost fully stretched because of the speed of the bat. The upper body is straightened again like in the basic position. The bodyweight is moved to the forward right leg.

Back to the basic position: Werner is preparing for the next stroke and moves back to the basic position **(6, 7)**.

Important (look at the enlarged pictures of the wrist):

A comparison of the position of the wrist in pictures 1, 3, 4 and 5 is well worth it. Here, Werner's wrist movement becomes very clear and that is the most important feature in the movement of the backhand topspin. In other words, all movements might be right, but if the movement of the wrist is too slow or too late, the dream of a successful backhand topspin is finished and the stroke is a failure.

Pictures to emphasize the importance of the use of the wrist:

Neutral position of the wrist: easy and
relaxed, the wrist is slightly bent down
so that the thumb and the forearm are
in line. The head of the bat points forward.

Backswing: the hand is bent down and
back at the wrist. The head of the bat points
backwards and down.

Forward movement: the wrist is moved fast,
forward and up.

At the end of the **follow-through,** the wrist is
back in neutral position.

Picture series 6: Stroke Combination of a Short Backhand Push and Backhand Topspin with Three Variations

Werner is demonstrating here how he is playing three different backhand topspins following a short push return:

- Variation 1: powerful backhand topspin over the table from the forehand side **(10-14)**.
- Variation 2: controlled backhand topspin from the backhand side away from the table **(10a-15a)**.
- Variation 3: extremely hard backhand topspin away from the table from the backhand side **(10b-15b)**.

A top player is characterized by being able to play a certain stroke technique from different positions with different targets (placement, speed, spin, flight path). The higher the ability to vary the strokes, the more difficult it is for a player to work out the opponent. Werner is one of these players who is able to use numerous variations.

Starting situation (1-9): Werner's opponent returns the ball to the middle of the forehand. He takes one big step forward with his right leg to meet the ball above the table just after the bounce (1-3). It has to be a ball with backspin because Werner answers with a short parallel push. His bat angle is slightly open at the moment of contact with the ball (4). Werner's return is very short (6) and he moves his right leg back to get into a stroke position. He gets there with one more extra step **(7, 8, 9, 10)**.

Variation 1 (10-14): Then he moves toward the medium long return of his opponent when he puts the right leg in front **(11)** and gets ready for the stroke. He brings the shoulder and elbow of the playing arm forward and creates the necessary tension in the arm and shoulder muscles. *Picture 12* shows Werner at the end of the backswing. His bodyweight is on his forward right leg. Elbow and shoulder are extremely far forward and the wrist is slightly bent backwards. All of this points toward a very powerful backhand topspin with a lot of speed. The whole dynamic of the topspin becomes clear in **picture 13**. At the moment of making contact with the ball, Werner takes off with both his feet, and his playing arm is almost fully stretched. He hits the ball above the table. The forward right leg carries the movement of the stroke **(14)**.

Variation 2 (10a-15a): This time the return comes to Werner's backhand side. With a little parallel jump, he gets into a position a bit farther away from the table **(10a, 11a)**. The coming ball should have topspin. Werner is standing parallel. His backswing comparable to variations 1 and 3, but considerably shorter **(13a)**. He hits the ball in front of his body and only seems to intend a controlled return **(14a)**. This becomes clear because of his short backswing **(15a)**. The backhand topspin variety of Werner is mainly played with the wrist and a short forearm movement. He wants to keep the ball in play.

Variation 3 (10b-15b): Also in this variation, the opponent places a topspin ball to Werner's backhand. Werner jumps backwards into the ready position **(10b, 11b)**. In **picture 12b,** he starts the backswing for a topspin. **Picture 13b** shows him at the end of the backswing. Despite his parallel feet, he has moved his shoulder and elbow extremely far forward. An extremely hard backhand topspin follows, which has parts of a smash **(14b)**. In this case, we are talking about a *smash-spin.* The outstretched arm at the end of the follow-through stresses that this must be the final stroke.

Variation 1

Variation 2

Variation 3

Variation 2

Variation 3

3.8 Flip

"The flip is the most difficult stroke in table tennis"

The flip is a special stroke that returns short balls, especially short placed serves. It is played as a smash spin against balls with side spin and without spin, and as a mini topspin with the forearm against backspin and side-backspin balls. Sometimes the flip was the deciding factor in a game, either for or against the player who flipped because the flip has a high risk, and is only successful when the spin of the coming ball is read correctly.

*The word **flip** is derived from English and means **to snap your fingers** or to **turn over a plate or a pancake**. What has that got to do with the name for a table tennis technique? Nothing at first, but when you think about it, maybe a lot. In the same way as you snap your fingers or a cook throws up a pancake to turn it from one side to the other, you must use your wrist and forearm very speedily and short for a flip movement. What is important about the flip?*

A flip of high quality is the most difficult stroke in table tennis. The difficulty is to tackle the rotation of the coming ball, which you must recognize correctly. Additionally, you have got very little space for the movement because you must hit a short ball above the table. The countless possibilities of placing the ball and the endless stroke varieties make it very complex.

The flip is, as you said, a difficult special stroke that demands a lot of control over the ball and wrist movement. When did you learn it?

My father tried to teach me for weeks. When exactly that was, I can't remember. It certainly takes years to learn it perfectly.

Some players at the amateur level don't even know what a flip is. Is it possible to play table tennis successfully without a flip?

Sure, up to a certain level. But each stroke variety you can't play is limiting.

Werner flips dangerously, here together with his long term partner Karl Jindrak

The flip is an attacking stroke, which arose during the '70s and was then developed further. In which tactical situations is it used?

When you return a service and as a game opener.

What is the difference between a flip against backspin versus against topspin?

The possible flight path of a flip is relatively short when you return a serve. That means you must put a lot of topspin on the ball so that it doesn't go off. You must always consider the rotation of the coming ball, and the execution against topspin is easier than against backspin. The possible flight path for a parallel ball is the shortest, so this placement is the most difficult one.

When do you use a flip?

When I think it is necessary. It depends on the coming ball and the game situation, which can't generally be predicted.

*Some say that the flip is basically a mini topspin played with the wrist and the forearm. By now there is also the **"Chiquita" flip** as a sidespin variety. Then there is the smash flip as Ma Lin occasionally shows us. Which flip is suitable for which ball?*

Basically, every flip is suitable for each ball. The more spin you put on a ball, the more control you have over the ball. This makes the smash flip very difficult.

There is a high risk if you want to flip a short backspin serve. Isn't it easier to push the ball?

Not necessarily. Every player must find the best solution considering his own stroke consistency and the game situation.

Generally, the flip seems to have lost a bit of importance in comparison to the long aggressive push or a short return. You don't see soft flips any more because the opponent would make good use of it straight away and hard flips are very risky. If my judgement is right, why does every top player need a flip as one of their basic strokes?

The permanent change of table tennis sport in the direction of aggressiveness has also led to changes with the flip. I don't think that the flip has generally lost its meaning.

Some say that a backhand flip is more difficult than a forehand flip. Is that true?

I don't think that there is a big difference between them concerning complexity.

How do you train the flip? Can you give us a standard exercise?

The famous standard exercise is "short forehand-long backhand." A classic example is where the training partner returns my serve either short to my forehand or long to my backhand.

Did you ever win an important match with a flip? If yes, how and against whom?

The left-handed player Timo Boll is well-known for his flips

I played my most important flip against Kong Linghui in the semi-final of the World Championships tournament 2003. He had a match point and served a little bit too high, and I won the point directly with a flip.

Is there a player whose flips you dread?

Yes. It was no fun to play against Aleksandar Karakasevic from Serbia in the Mixed Doubles.

The one who can flip *has a clear advantage.*
I flip *when the moment is right.*
If somebody flips against me, *I loop.*
A flip in modern table tennis is *more important than ever.*
To flip at the right moment *often means a direct point.*
It is a challenge to win a direct point with a flip

▶ Picture series 7: Werner's backhand flip (9 pictures)

Werner is well-known for his precise flip game with a lot of control – especially with the backhand. In this picture series he shows us an aggressive backhand flip with a following forehand by jumping around to the backhand side.

Preparation and backswing: From a parallel basic position, Werner has recognized the short placement of the coming ball and shifts his bodyweight from the left **(1)** to the right leg **(2)**, so that he can push off with his right leg afterward **(3)**. He brings the front right leg forward to get into an optimal basic position to achieve good balance for the backhand flip. Simultaneously, he moves the bat toward his body for a backswing **(3)** so he can lean over the table to flip the short ball optimally. Werner's playing arm is bent at a right angle at the end of the backswing. Now the forward movement is starting.

Forward movement: Picture 4 shows Werner just before making contact with the ball. Especially at this moment of the stroke, the player needs optimal balance. In addition, despite the fact that the backhand flip is mainly executed with the forearm and wrist, Werner shows us how extremely explosive the backhand flip is and that the whole body is involved. Werner accelerates his bat fast, forward and up, when he makes contact with the ball **(compare 4 with 5)** and hits the ball at the end of the rising point at the peak of the bounce. It is also obvious that the bodyweight is shifted toward the right leg during the stroke **(4+5)**.

Follow through: At the end of the follow through Werner is stretching his playing arm far forward but it is not completely stretched. The bat is slightly closed. That hints at a flip with topspin. The comparison of picture 4 and 5 clearly shows the upward movement of the playing arm.

Follow-through and transition to the forehand topspin: Now Werner wants to take the bat back into the neutral position. He pushes off from the right leg and takes the left leg back at the same time **(6)**. In **picture 7**, it becomes clear that Werner prepares for a forehand stroke. His playing arm is already in the forehand position. The right foot takes off so that it can take the bodyweight during the backswing for a forehand topspin from the backhand side **(8)**. **Picture 9** shows clearly how Werner swings back for a forehand topspin from the backhand side to follow the offensive flip with a forehand topspin to continue the pressure on the opponent. This stroke combination should be a part of the standard repertoire of every offensive player. Werner can do this perfectly.

▶ **Picture series 8: Stroke Combination: Backhand Flip and Forehand Topspin**

This stroke combination shows that a top player must always be able to play from each position with the backhand and forehand. The backhand flip from the forehand side is one example. Additionally, a top player must be able to play good strokes in tricky or difficult situations. Werner demonstrates this impressively when he plays a speedy forehand topspin from a backhand position. If we compare the picture series, it becomes clear that Werner is in command of the main features of a forehand topspin with a flexible solution for his movement from a difficult starting position. The deciding point is what is happening at the moment of making contact with the ball.

Picture 1: Werner is standing in the basic position on the backhand side, slightly open, with parallel legs, the bat in the neutral position in front of his body and he is expecting the service.

Picture 2: He has noticed the placement of the serve (the ball can't yet be seen in the picture), then he pushes off with his left leg and takes the right leg forward in the direction of the forehand side.

Picture 3: He places his right foot down over the heel. The ball is placed short in the middle of the forehand.

Picture 4: He rolls the foot from the heel to the front and takes the bodyweight with the front of the foot. Simultaneously, he bends the right knee a lot so he can move the body over the right leg to play a backhand flip from the forehand side.

Picture 5: The whole dynamic and aggression of this flip are underlined by the nearly outstretched playing arm and the jump with both legs at the end of the stroke.

Picture 6: Werner is in an extreme position at the table, which means far in the forehand side. The bodyweight is now on the right leg.

Picture 7: He pushes off with the right leg to get back to the table.

Picture 8: He straightens up and starts a parallel jump.

Picture 9: The jump is nearly finished, but the right leg is in front. That could indicate that Werner wants to play one more backhand.

Picture 10: But the ball is placed to Werner's forehand, and he plays a forehand topspin from this inconvenient position. Speedily, he shifts his bodyweight to the left leg so that he can take the right leg backwards.

Picture 11: Despite the poor position to the ball and time pressure, Werner succeeds in playing a powerful forehand topspin with optimal stroke movement.

Picture 12: At the end of the stroke, Werner has caught his bodyweight and the strong forward impulse on the front left leg. The back right leg stabilizes the balance.

Picture 13/14: Werner moves back into the playing position, which is slightly backwards because of the stroke.

3.9   Block

"Many final hits are prepared by cleverly placed blocks"

The block is the answer to topspin balls. In extreme situations, a smash is also blocked by a reflexive holding movement. Just like the topspin has been further developed as the most important offensive weapon (also through further development of the material), many inventive offensive players found clever new block varieties as solutions. The classical holding block where the player just adjusts the angle of the bat against the coming topspin just after the bounce is still the basic form of the block, but active blocks (like the drive-block or the counter-block) are very special varieties in modern top table tennis. Backspin, side-backspin or even sidespin and stop blocks are very special varieties that not every player is in command of. Altogether, the block is underestimated by many players concerning its meaning.

Without a block, you are nothing, Mario Amizic, one of the most successful coaches in the world and Butterfly Sports Director, once said. How important is the block really for an attacking player?

I think he is completely right. The block on the backhand side is an important stroke form. You hardly block with the forehand. Today, you try to loop against it.

Many books differentiate between many different block varieties: the passive holding block, the drive block, the active counter topspin block with forearm and wrist, the backspin block and the stop block against high balls. Could you briefly describe the differences of the varieties?

Basically, the varieties a player is using often should be more important. The backspin block is very effective but also very difficult and therefore very risky. It is very suitable for players who like to take risks, like the French Damien Eloi. The passive holding block should not be played so much because the opponent takes the initiative. The active spin or drive block is far more suitable to modern table tennis because you can put your opponent under pressure. Every player should be able to play the stop block.

Which block variety is the most important in your game and when do you use it?

I use the active spin and drive block regularly.

There was a time when the holding block seemed to be out, but recently you can see the Chinese block the ball (sometimes passively) by just holding the bat against the ball. What do you think about this block?

In this case, the block is probably only used because the opponent is too far away from the table. As a tactical means, it is still useful.

From a tactical point of view, many players are getting mixed up when they think the one who blocks is passive. Especially at top level, the block situation can be turned into a very aggressive and active situation. Do you know of such game situations and can you describe them?

At the top level, players are very conscious about the effectiveness of the block varieties. I use the block often against weaker players to take it easy. That way you can win a match without a lot of physical effort.

Quite often you hear a player cursing: "I can't block one ball!" or "I don't have any control and block everything into the woods!" And indeed, it is often that offensive players fail in their weak blocking game and not with their attacks. What role does the block game play for you from a psychological-tactical point of view?

It happens quite often that, for different reasons (for example nervousness in close situations), you forget about your strength, the offensive game. That means you try to win points with your weaknesses. Naturally, that is rarely successful. To prevent that from happening, you should always be aware of your strengths and weaknesses.

It is probably my imagination, but in some cases it seems that players who are afraid really can't block one ball on the table. Is the reason for that the very fine technique of the block where you have to take it easy and be relaxed?

The problem is the lack of self-confidence, and with that, the growing fear to make mistakes. The fear works like a blockage. That way, the active block very soon becomes a passive block.

Blocking also requires a good ability to anticipate. On the one hand, a special placement is expected and on the other hand, the power and the spin of the stroke are anticipated. Can that be trained?

Naturally, the most important factor in table tennis is training. The more often you play against or with a player, the easier it is to anticipate his strokes.

Are there players who are extremely good at blocking?

The Belarusian Vladimir Samsonov is among other things a gifted block player.

In training sessions with children, exercises with topspin and blocking are not always the most popular ones. They all want to loop but blocking is (perhaps slightly exaggerated) a bit too boring for most of them. How can I motivate such players to exercise the block with more concentration.

If I play the passive role during exercises, I look at it as my duty to make as few mistakes as possible.

Werner's active backhand block

I expect the same from my training partner when I play the active part. When I was a junior, it wasn't easy for me either.

How do you personally feel when blocking, do you like it?

I like to block, but I like looping even more.

Where is the optimal place for a block: above the table, when the ball is rising or behind the table?

During the second quarter of the rising phase, I have the best control.

Roughly, how many of the points (in regards to percentage) at the top level are won by blocks today?

Statistics have a better answer for that. Probably not so many, but many final strokes are prepared by active block balls.

If a younger player were to ask you how he could improve his block game, what would you answer?

Only by training very hard.

If you can block, *it is easy for you.*
The best often *fail* when blocking.
If I block poorly, *I should counter loop.*
If I win by blocking, *I should continue.*
The training of a block *is not exhausting.*
Blocking is *an important part of my game.*

3.10 Backspin Defence

"With a backspin defence, you sometimes can change the course of a match."

Generally, the backspin defence is a defensive stroke technique where topspin balls and sometimes also smashes can be answered with backspin more or less far away from the table. Because the number of defensive players has gone down drastically at all levels (among the top 50 in the world there are just about four male defenders), many players think that this stroke technique is of no importance. Instead the truth is far from that, because in certain game situations, you can see that many top players sometimes use a backspin defence successfully. Generally, a game between an attacker and a defender is very popular among the spectators because the rallies are often extremely spectacular. In the future, the defensive game should receive more attention. At the moment, the best defender in the world is the Korean Joo Se Hyuk.

The technique we are talking about now is surely not one of your best techniques, but you can surely play it. I am talking about the backspin defence. Did that ever play a special role in your table tennis career?

For my game, the backspin defence only played a minor role, even though you sometimes might change the course of a match with it.

Genius players like the Swede Jan-Ove Waldner or the Pole Andrzej Grubbe didn't mind playing backspin defence balls in certain game situations to surprise their opponents. I think I have seen you too playing such balls. When does it make sense to play such a ball?

The backspin defence ball only makes sense for offensive players in certain game situations. The purposeful use of a different game system doesn't make sense.

Defending with a normal rubber is technically very difficult. What is so difficult about it?

The bat of an attacker must have blade and rubbers that are very fast. Therefore, it is difficult to have enough control when you defend. With slow rubbers, you can also defend consistently.

It is easier to defend with long pimples. What is the reason for that?

Long pimples are used with a thin sponge or no sponge at all, which decreases the speed and increases control. Rubbers with pimples are not so vulnerable against spin. As I said, the difficulty is in controlling fast blade rubber combinations.

Joo Se Hyuk, the defense specialist from South Korea, lost against Werner in the final 2003

The long backspin defence is equally difficult concerning the coordination of the whole body as the topspin. Still, experts maintain that defenders need more control and fine coordination than offensive players. What is your opinion?

I don't think that it is a question of control but a question of training. Both are very complex movements that must be practiced often.

Do you sometimes play defence just for fun or even use a defensive bat?

I enjoy playing a defensive ball every now and again just to get more feeling for my material. Changing the bat for that would be counterproductive.

How could you see that a talented youngster is more suitable for the defensive game?

I think, primarily, it is a question of the player's personality. You will hardly advise a player to play defence if he is not doing it already.

Is this expression right: "The one who can push well is also able to play defence with backspin?"

It will certainly be easier for him than for somebody who has problems with pushing already.

On which side is it more difficult to defend? Some say defenders are weaker on the forehand side.

When defending with the forehand, more muscle groups must be coordinated than for the backhand, so the stroke is probably more difficult to learn. But to say generally that defenders are weaker on the forehand side, I think, is wrong.

Today, the backspin defence hardly plays a role in the basic education of the player. Is that the reason why there are so few defenders in Europe?

I don't think that the backspin defence needs to be part of the basic education of attackers. Instead I think that the rule changes of the past years have made it nearly impossible for a classical defender without a strong attacking stroke to keep up internationally.

But also at the amateur level, there are fewer and fewer backspin experts. Isn't that boring for table tennis?

Rule changes that reduce variety must lead to less complexity. The sport doesn't necessarily become more boring because of that. It is still possible to move up right to the top as a modern defender.

How can you see if there is a lot of backspin on a defensive ball or not?

The noise, the flight path and sometimes the stamp on the ball. A lot of experience makes the estimation easier.

Is it true that some professionals sometimes play defence during training sessions to improve their control of the ball and their coordination?

Yes, some professionals do that. I can't say if many are doing it. I certainly enjoy it.

Is there a defender who really impressed you?

The Chinese Xin Hua, "The Smiler," was, until the mid '90s, a real player personality.

The few remaining defenders of world class are all playing with long pimples on the backhand and short pimples inside on the forehand. The best defender at the moment is Joo Se Hyuk from South Korea (your opponent in the final in Paris 2003). What made his backspin defence so dangerous?

It was not the quantity of his spin varieties but the consistency of his defence and his dangerous attacks, which characterize the last remaining defenders.

I only play backspin defence
for fun or in an emergency situation.
Against backspin defence balls, *I use my head.*
Backspin defence *is cool to watch.*
Children should *not underestimate* backspin defence strokes
in their effect.
I really like backspin defence strokes with long pimples.
Offensive players *often can't estimate* backspin defence strokes *correctly.*

3.11   Balloon Defence

"A balloon defence is extreme."

The opposite of the backspin defence, the balloon defence is played with topspin. Topspin players also manage to play balloon balls with sidespin and, in certain situations, also with side-backspin. The balls have a very high flight path, and the players are a long way away from the table when they play the stroke. Smash-balloon duels are very fun for spectators because of their extreme dynamic. Tactically, balloon balls are used by offensive players in emergency situations when a player is forced away from the table and doesn't have a chance to play an effective counter topspin. Defensive players use it

95

consciously to change the spin. Good balloon balls may force the attacker to make a mistake when smashing these high balls with a lot of spin. In this way, missed balloon balls have sometimes turned a game around. A missed balloon ball is comparable to a missed penalty, especially when it is 10:10 in the deciding set.

The balloon defence is equally as fascinating as the smash and especially breathtaking for spectators. What are your balloon abilities like?

I think, quite good.

A brilliant balloon expert was the Polish world class player Andrzej Grubba, who sadly died far too early. Some Butterfly blades have been named after him. Surely you had to play against his balloon defence, which he could play equally good with his forehand and backhand. How did you cope with that?

I only played once against him. It was during a team competition at a European Championship. I didn't have any problems with his balloon defence, but his tricky serve made life difficult for me. I just couldn't see if he was serving with or without backspin, which often forced me to take defensive actions.

Two further balloon artists are without doubt the Belgian Jean-Michel Saive and the Swedish table tennis legend Jan-Ove Waldner, who again and again annoyed and sometimes made their opponents desperate with high balls. What do these players, who like to move away from the table, do to master this stroke perfectly?

They definitely need to be physically very fit, which is the basis for extraordinary success with defensive balls. Additionally, you need a lot of experience to look ahead and react, and a lot of practice for consistency of course.

You said before your balloon defence was quite good. Could you improve it?

Naturally, I could improve my consistency for balloon defence a lot by training. But it is not part of my standard tactic, therefore I am not going to invest much time in it.

Is the topspin technique a presupposition for good balloon balls?

Not necessarily, but the forward rotation decides the flight path of the ball.

Jean-Michel Saive, the former European Champion from Belgium, gets the spectators going with his spectacular balloon balls.

What are the spin variations for balloon balls?

Everything is allowed. Practically, you would use side-topspin most of the time and rarely side-backspin.

A well-known coach said once that every training session should include a balloon exercise, not because of the technique but because you train coordination, speed and control of the ball, reaction and awareness of space, and it's simply fun. Do you also do that and, if yes, how often?

Not regularly, just when I feel like it, previously more, now less. My training as an older player is more target directed.

What is the difference between a good and bad balloon ball?

The good balloon balls are played with a lot of rotation, as long as possible to the baseline and to the side.

What makes the balloon ball so magical and fascinating to spectators and table tennis fans?

It is an extreme ball. The ball is extremely fast and flies a long way with extreme rotation. The players must really exhaust themselves and go long. Extremes are always nice to watch.

From the tactical point of view, the balloon defence is more of an emergency stroke, which is used when the player is moved away from the table and doesn't have another choice to play the ball. It is also possible that players at the amateur level use the balloon ball consciously, if they notice that their opponent has trouble with winning on high balls. In which situations do you play balloon balls, and do you know current top players who consciously play balloon balls?

At the professional level, it is only used as an emergency stroke, even by somebody like Jean-Michel Saive, who has turned halls into madhouses with his artistry. Hardly any professional is insecure against balloon balls. Using the balloon ball at lower levels as a tactic is possible but too risky at professional level.

Perhaps my impression is wrong, but the Chinese don't very often play balloon balls. Is that perhaps because of their different and more aggressive game philosophy?

Possibly, but probably they don't need an emergency stroke as often as we do.

If you think about technical basic education, when should a child learn the balloon defence stroke: right from the beginning or at a later time?

I don't think that a minimum age makes sense.

When did you learn the balloon stroke?

Werner gets with his backhand under the ball to lift it up

The balloon stroke was one of my first stroke techniques.

What should a player definitely take care of when he answers a balloon ball with a smash?

You should take your time and prepare the smash well. Watch the flight path and the bounce on your own half of the table.

When does it make sense to answer a balloon ball with a stop block and what do you have to think of?

When the opponent is far away from the table, then you only need to hold the bat passively so that the existing rotation can be used. But be careful, if you judge the rotation incorrectly, your stop block might end up as a flop!

The best balloon defence player is *surely not the best attacker.*
If you can play a balloon ball, *you have a solution.*
In table tennis, balloon balls are *the last straw in defence.*
I am fully concentrating against balloon defence.
I play balloon defence *and run away from the table.*

4

4 TECHNIQUE AND TRAINING OF TECHNIQUE

"Technical perfection is not a presupposition to become World Champion."

Techniques in table tennis are forms of movement, which are designed to solve certain tasks in a game. Here we differentiate between **stroke** *and* **footwork technique.** *During technical training, these techniques are learned, stabilized and made automatic. These so-called basic techniques are constantly differentiated in training so that the player learns more varieties of the basic technique. The more varieties and the more consistent the execution of the technical repertoire of a player, the better he will be able to solve the complex situations he encounters in table tennis. Therefore, technique in table tennis is definitely one of the basic factors for success. There are of course other factors, like tactics, fitness and psychology, as well as other influencing factors from the outside on top of these.*

Technique is one of the main terms in table tennis. "He has got a brilliant tech- nique!" "He has got a weird technique!" "He is playing with a good technique!" "Look at his weird technique, yet he still gets the ball on the table with it!" These and many other similar exclamations about technique can be heard everywhere. However, the point still is, "He must work a lot more on his technique!" What exactly is technique for you in table tennis and how important is technical ability for being successful?

It is very important to play with an efficient technique because success depends directly upon it. The more efficient my stroke or footwork technique is, the more physical energy I can save. The more techniques I can master, the better I am prepared for the balls coming from my opponent.

For new beginners, the learning of the different stroke techniques is very important so they are able to play the game. How did you learn your first techniques and what role did your father, as your first coach, play?

Mario Amizic, Butterfly Sports Director and new head coach at the Werner-Schlager-Academy, is known as one of the most successful coaches in the world.

You learn the basic techniques very quickly with a lot of training. The deciding question is which basic techniques are the right ones. My father had the gift of realizing that table tennis was then developing from long movements far away from the table to short movements close to the table. My successful and explosive game close to the table is due to his training.

By the way, how important is a good coach for technical training during the first years or is it possible to learn the techniques yourself?

Theoretically, it might be possible to learn to play table tennis at a world class level on your own. However, you would invest too much time and energy in mental dead ends and lose motivation very quickly because of that. To improve technically, you must recognize the problem, define it and find a solution. Defining the problem is still easy; for example, play the ball from position A to position B. Finding a suitable solution without experience is more difficult, as is recognizing problems. Identifying future problems is the most difficult task. After that, the most time-consuming job follows, which is the transfer and adaptation of the solution to the problem for you. A good and experienced coach can concentrate on the main points; this is the transfer of stroke, footwork and ideally also mental techniques specifically for you. These basic techniques are the basis for everything you learn at a later stage and are therefore very important. Changing a technique after a few years is almost impossible.

Can you remember which techniques you learned very quickly and which ones were difficult?

In the beginning, it was easier to play with my forehand than to play backhand. Later that changed because I had problems in improving shifting weight during my forehand technique. This problem is still not completely resolved.

When did you start with "many balls practice" and why is this training method absolutely necessary for technical training?

My father used "many balls practice" right from the beginning. The advantage is the efficiency of training because you have many repetitions of the stroke in a short time. You can work more intensively with a problem.

What do you think of the so-called control exercises with counting, which means 15 x forehand topspin against block without making a mistake, hit and return are counted?

Consistency exercises are a good opportunity to practice the mental endurance in addition to the technique. Who doesn't know the situation where you lose your nerves and make a mistake just before reaching the finish line? As a junior, I wasn't a very consistent player. Therefore, I didn't like exercises where you had to play 20 forehand loops.

When you are learning a technique, you always have a target technique in your mind. Maybe you got it from other better players or your coach explained them to you. How did you achieve this or whom did you copy?

From world class players of course! Especially concerning the serves. Why bother to reinvent the wheel when there are so many successful "wheels" around? The adaptation of these personally tuned techniques demands enough sweat already. You may fail with some techniques, but you shouldn't get discouraged by this. In my experience, there is no problem that can't be resolved. There is only too little time.

At the top level, you frequently see the use of a video camera to correct mistakes. Players can see their own mistakes and then try to correct them. How important were videos to you? Have you got special experiences with that?

Sadly, I could not pay for a video camera during my time as a junior. Perhaps I realized the value of video analysis very late. Today, I am very grateful for this help and use it intensively.

Training with a robot is also described as being very effective. Did you practice with a robot and what are your experiences?

Similar to a ball box, the robot gives you a good way to work on your technique and improve it. Later, during my junior time, my father could afford one and we used it regularly. It was also good because you could practice alone.

You have been playing table tennis for 30 years now, half of that time at the top level. Every professional I have talked to says that they could improve on one or another technique. What are you working with at the moment? Which technique can you improve?

At the moment, I am working on my problem with distance. I also optimize constantly. You must continuously adapt to new trends (like new serve varieties). I very often get the feeling that I get worse automatically if I spend a long time working on one problem more intensively. As long as I improve altogether, that is okay. Table tennis is a very individual sport, especially because each technique is executed slightly differently by each player. Even at the top level, you can see great differences; some players, for example, play a topspin with a very long movement, but others play it with a very short movement. There are some players with techniques from out of the book and others with a very individual style.

Which category do you belong to (if possible, give specific examples)?

I see myself as one of those players with a very individual technique. I think at the top level there can't be players with a perfect technique because strength or weakness is defined mainly by individuality.

You say that there are no players, who play exactly according to the book at the top level. Are you not exaggerating a bit?

No, from my point of view, there are no players like that. In the books, you will not find individual strengths and weaknesses, and therefore there are no top players who play according to the techniques in a book. But there are some players who play closer to that than others. Generally, you can say Asians play closer to the books than Europeans.

Who are the greatest individualists and who deviates most?

Each world class player became world class through his individuality. Everybody has a special weapon. Timo Boll's topspin (played almost only with the forearm) is such a special weapon. It's very effective, but it can't be played by everybody.

A basic question with technical training is to decide whether the technique is wrong or whether is it an individual style. This becomes especially clear when you look at the grips, for example, of Kreanga, Chila, Eloi and also Timo Boll when he is returning the serve (the index finger is right in the middle of his backhand side). If you were the coach, when would you interfere and correct?

The German National Women's Coach, Joerg Bitzigeio with multi balls training.

I would interfere if I could see that it is a definite disadvantage now or for the future.

What should be the leading principle for a coach when correcting the technique?

Essentially, everything that is leading to success in the long run should be allowed.

Last autumn, you played as the first professional for a longer period without fresh gluing. What were your experiences and why did you stop the trial?

My technique is too complex for changing it as a whole in a short while. I underestimated the complexity. I learned a lot about my game through that.

Could you comment on the statement by a renowned coach who said "You can't win a game with a perfect technique alone?"

Surely that is directed toward the importance of the mental constitution of a player. If you lose your nerves, you can't apply a perfect technique.

Technical training for me is *like daily bread.*
Technical clean players *are easy to work out.*
Technical training at the age of 35 *is still fun.*
When fresh gluing is forbidden, technique becomes
more important than ever.
A good coach *corrects technical mistakes permanently.*
Technical perfection *is no presupposition to becoming a world champion.*

5

5 PLAYING SYSTEMS IN TABLE TENNIS

"If you want to develop your playing systems further, you should learn from the top players."

In soccer, the playing system is easy to understand: 4-4-2, 4-3-3, etc. In table tennis, the term playing system is more like the way of playing. Either there are different main strokes that decide the playing system of a player or the more active or passive game philosophy decides that. The active player wants to win the point himself, whereas the passive player waits for the mistake of the opponent. The main stroke of the offensive player is the topspin, the defensive player uses backspin. These main strokes are then combined with all the other techniques in different degrees. Today, you can find very aggressive offensive players in top table tennis but also those who are very strong in blocking and allow the opponent to attack. Today, defensive players must be able to take the initiative with a strong forehand topspin. Pure block or drive players are only found in women's table tennis. Analyzing the way a player plays has become a lot more difficult during the last decade because the topspin players have become more complete and are more difficult to work out.

In the lower levels, it is relatively easy to differentiate between different playing systems. The players are more limited in their technical abilities. You will find the classical block or drive players, the passive all-around player (who pushes a lot), and the passive defenders (who only wait for a mistake by their opponent). These playing systems don't exist any longer in men's top table tennis. Which playing systems can be found?

You can roughly differentiate between an active and a passive playing system, whereas the classical defender with a purely passive defence is gone. The ones I call "modern defenders" are all in command of strong attacking strokes. Well-known players in this category are the South Korean Joo Se Hyuk and the Austrian Chen Weixing. My active offensive colleagues are all only slightly different from each other concerning their aggressiveness. Block and drive players are also gone. In short, you could say an aggressive, offensive component becomes more and more important. In women's table tennis, you can see the same development, but it hasn't progressed as far yet.

The majority of Asian top players are now playing with shake-hand grip, like the triple World Champion Wang Liquin from China (r.) and the number one from South Korea, Oh Sang Eun (l.).

How would you explain your playing system to the reader?

Game: aggressive and offensive with backhand and forehand
Strength: ability to adapt easily, a lot of varieties
Weaknesses: consistency
Special abilities: mental strength through experience

At the top level in the world, individual offensive systems are clearly dominant. There are only three defensive players among the top 50. Timo Boll, Vladimir Samsonov, Ma Lin and Wang Liqin are offensive players and still very different in their individual playing systems. Could you explain the playing systems of these players, looking at their main characteristics and differences?

Timo and Vladi are nearly the same from my point of view. Both have services with a lot of variety and good control of the ball, especially when returning it. Timo relies more on his forehand when attacking than Vladi, who uses both sides equally. Timo is able to play more aggressively than Vladi, whereas Vladi (also through experience) is more consistent. Wang Liqin profits more from his training quantity and his extreme physical fitness than from a good hand. He plays with little variation but is extremely aggressive and consistent. I think Ma Lin is the player with most varieties. That is why he often has problems making the right decisions. He plays with the penholder grip and has the tricky choice between the "old" penholder backhand (played with the forehand side of the bat) and the "new" penholder backhand (played with the backhand side of the bat).

After the 2008 Olympic Games in Beijing, gluing will be forbidden. Will there perhaps be new developments, and which playing system will be the future?

The current tendency toward more speed will remain. As soon as the players get used to the new material, the average spectator will not notice a difference. The players will compensate the slower material with more physical fitness.

Even if there are more penholder players in Asia, there are still many excellent penholder players right at the top of the World Ranking List. How do you look at the competition of grip in connection with the playing systems?

I can't see a competition there. Every grip has its advantages and disadvantages. The penholder game became more attractive again by the new backhand option, the penholder backhand loop.

Does playing with the left or right hand influence the playing system of a player?

Partially. Nearly all left-handed players have the same playing system. The right-handed players are not influenced at all.

At what time did you develop your playing system and were there certain factors influencing you (coaches, idols, own ideas, etc.)?

My playing system is a result of my father's imagination, which I permanently try to improve and extend. This development happens also when watching my idols.

If you were to advise a young talented player concerning the development of his individual playing system, what advice could you give?

Individual playing systems need individual advice. Individuality only means "advantage for a limited period." The real genius will try to outlast time.

If you don't have a playing system, *you can't win in the long run.*
If you want to develop your playing system,
you should learn from the professionals.
The playing system of the future *will be even faster.*
The playing system of a player shows *his understanding of the game.*
Differentiating playing systems in table tennis *become more and more difficult.*

⑥ TACTICS AND COACHING

"A winning tactic that you can talk about but can't use is worthless."

Tactics in table tennis are a central and deciding component. The player tries to adapt his game in such a way to the opponent that he has an advantage and wins. He actively tries to force his game onto the opponent. In a passive role, he tries to prevent the opponent from active moves and tries to enforce errors. The tactical ability of a player is mainly decided by his technical ability and his mental strength. In table tennis, the coach has the special role of watching the player tactically before, during and after the match.

Tactics *is a term that is used by all but is understood differently. In some cases, tactics start before the match, while others understand tactics as a certain playing sequence. How do you explain tactics?*

My understanding of tactics is the adaptation of your own playing system to that of your opponent. Some also stress that it is the "psychological warfare" with which you try to make your opponent insecure, often starting before the match. Generally, on a basic level these behaviour patterns are often successful. Among world class players, it is considered to be unfair and rarely successful.

How do you prepare yourself tactically before a match?

a) *If you know your opponent:*
   Before the match, the tactics are discussed with your coach. During the match, they are adapted according to your form on the day.
b) *If you have never played against that opponent before:*
   You try to get as much information about your opponent before the match and then discuss the tactics with your coach. During the match, the tactics are adapted according to your form on the day.
c) *If you have played against your opponent many times before and you know each other very well:*
   During the match, the tactics are adapted according to your form on the day.

The coach as a source of information: Werner Schlager's long term coach Ferenc Karsai.

How important is the role of the coach when deciding about the tactics? How much should the player decide or should he even make the decisions alone? Is it dependent upon age?

You can't answer this question in general. First of all, the character, the player's ability to communicate, and the coach are deciding factors that form the basis of information from which you create the tactics. If you take it as a fact that older people can communicate better then you could consider the influence of the player is depending on his age. A main point to the question of tactics is the ability of the player to put it into practice. A winning tactic that you can talk about but can't use is worthless. That is the real strength of a good coach.

If you are playing a match today, how much do you communicate with your coach Ferenc Karsai and what do you expect of him during the match concerning tactics?

I look at my coach as a supplier of information. The more information I get, the more profound my tactical decisions will be.

Let's assume you are playing a match and recognize that your tactics are wrong. How quickly do you change your tactics and how important is the role of the coach in such a situation?

You react right away of course. The coach can use the time until the next break to prepare an alternative tactic.

During the World Championships 2003 when you sensationally became World Champion, you had to get through some tricky situations in the quarterfinals against Wang Liqin and Kong Linghui in the semifinals when you were close to defeat. Were the big points planned or was it more intuition or a mixture of both?

So-called **"big points"** can't be planned. They happen or don't happen.

Which players do you think are tactical geniuses and what are their characteristics?

Those players who make the right decisions at the right time – consciously or unconsciously – are tactical geniuses.

A well-known coach told me once that there are players at the top level who play tactically undisciplined. How do you understand tactically "undisciplined" to mean?

You don't stick to the tactics you agreed to with your coach. From the point of view of the coach, another winning tactical variation of the player can also be called undisciplined. The final result should be the main point here.

Today, the game is so fast that the margin between offensive players is so small that tactical intuition becomes more and more important. What does tactical intuition mean to you and how can it be developed?

The faster you play, the more important subconscious tactical decisions become. Intuition is always a deciding factor. The brain is soon overcharged with the processing of information and can and should only define the borderlines where you react automatically. Sport psychology is recommended for the development of the necessary self-confidence.

Too many tactics can prevent a player, especially when he is young, from developing his own game. How far can tactics go so that they are not too restrictive?

It is the job of a coach to prevent this from happening.

When did your father start to study and teach you tactics consciously?

The understanding of tactics is developed constantly through a lot of competition.

How long did it take you to become a tactically "clever" player?

That is difficult to answer because it is all a question of your personal estimation and therefore relative. You definitely need a lot of experience to become a tactically clever player.

Your coach gives you tactical advice for a certain serve during a time out. Do you follow it, ignore it or are you even angry?

It depends on the situation. If I am convinced that the advice is good then I will do it.

Which tactical advice can you give against a left-handed offensive player?

None. There are no tips that apply in general. It is, for example, always dependent upon my own abilities.

Tactical understanding is *often early visible.*
To learn tactics is *not difficult but playing them is very difficult.*
Tactical tips *can't be given by everybody.*
You can make the biggest tactical mistake *and win despite it!*
The greatest tactical achievement *is often gained subconsciously!*
In table tennis, tactics are essential!

Picture series 9: Flexible, Fast Reaction and Unconventional Play

The following game situation is proof of Werner's flexible, speedy and unconventional way of playing because it shows two situations that follow the motto to make the best out of a certain situation. In other words, he is trying to play the best possible ball in an unfavorable situation. His opponent, in this case Timo Boll, could also make a mistake.

Pictures 1-6: Werner serves in his typical manner with the forehand from the backhand side. He plays the ball with backspin short to Timo's forehand (left-handed player).

Pictures 7-9: Timo takes the backspin ball very early and puts it back parallel to Werner's forehand. Picture 9 does not tell us anything about the length of the ball. It seems that Werner wants to take the short to half-long return with his backhand.

Pictures 10-17: Something different happens. Werner has probably noticed that the ball is long enough to play a forehand topspin and prepares (although his right leg is in front) for a topspin with a lot of spin, which he places in Timo's forehand. This forehand topspin is

- flexible, because he plays it from an unfavorable position
- a quick reaction because it results out of a new situation – the return is longer than expected
- unconventional, because the exceptional situation (change of intention) demands an exceptional solution of movement

Pictures 18-20: Timo, a champion of counter topspins, estimates the spin of Werner's topspin correctly and loops the ball with a clever placement right on Werner's elbow. That means that the player must decide whether he returns the ball with his forehand or backhand. In picture 20, Werner still holds the bat as if he wants to return the ball with his backhand. Picture 21 shows Werner already using his forehand.

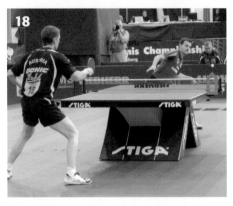

Pictures 21-25: If we compare pictures 21, 22 and 23, we recognize that Timo has played the ball toward a tricky place. Werner is holding his bat passively with the forehand and places the ball parallel toward the middle of the table by Timo. He

moves with his upper body toward the backhand side to be able to hit the ball better. He also hits the ball relatively late. Obviously, he didn't have a chance to play a more active stroke because of Timo's brilliant placement. But he keeps the ball in play despite his passive block and there is always the chance that the opponent might make a mistake.

Pictures 26-30: Timo doesn't make this mistake. He loops hard with his forehand toward the middle of the table, while Werner is ready at the middle of the table for the return. Who won the point in the end is unknown. Picture 30 doesn't tell us but indicates a return by Werner with the forehand.

7 DOUBLES

"Doubles demand compromise."

The demands of the singles and the doubles are completely different for the players. The players must hit the ball alternately, so the spaces and the movements are different. From a tactical point of view, the opening in the doubles is basically different because the service must be diagonal. The doubles partners must agree on their tactics and support each other psychologically and mentally. They are a team. For the spectators, the doubles are still fun to watch although there are tendencies that top players don't start in the doubles event at big tournaments so they can rest a bit more.

Doubles, some love it, but others can do without it. What do you think about doubles?

I really enjoy playing doubles. For me, it is a challenge to play with somebody else and find a winning strategy together.

Didn't your personal rise in professional table tennis begin with the doubles? You and your former Austrian doubles partner Karl Jindrak, who is now one of the ITTF Tournament directors, were among the most successful doubles in the pro tour. Didn't you become European Champions in 2005? Did the successes in the doubles encourage you for the singles?

In the beginning, yes. I had my first international success already as a cadet player. Later, I could follow my doubles successes in the singles, and now I look at the doubles as an interesting change that I enjoy playing.

What was so special about your combination? From the outside, Karl didn't look particularly fit during the last years.

We have been partners for a long time so we knew our strengths and weaknesses very well. Karl's strengths were his brilliant serves and his dangerous forehand. His weakness was in the physical areas, which wasn't so noticeable in the doubles.

Service in a doubles games

In St. Petersburg, you helped the Dutch player Trinko Keen to the nicest farewell present because the 38-year-old is now leaving the international stage. How did you manage to get to the finals?

To be honest, I didn't have great expectations. But already in the first Game, everything went surprisingly well. It was surprising because we played several years ago together in the pro tour and got to the semifinals, but we didn't work well together. This time it was different. We played better together from game to game and got to the final. It was an interesting and happy experience.

Why couldn't you win after a well-deserved lead of 3:1 in the final against Timo Boll/Christian Suess, losing 4:3 in the end?

Boll/Suess were the only doubles who could play at the same level as us. In the sixth, set they had luck on their side with three lucky balls in a row. In the deciding seventh set, Suess played from 3:6 onward without a mistake.

What is special about a good doubles player in general?

A good doubles player must agree about tactics with his partner.

Why is the combination of a left-handed and right-handed player the best combination in an attacking game?

The combination "left-right" has the advantage of a good service of the left-handed player plus no general "weaker side" (the backhand). Also the paths of movement cross less, which means the players are less often in each others' way especially after the service.

When two offensive right-handed players play together what must they be aware of?

They should possess a good doubles serve and the server must rotate quickly after his serve, toward an optimal neutral position.

When two left-handed players play together what must they do?

Surprising victory with the Dutchman Trinko Keen at the European Championships 2008 in St. Petersburg.

They must take care that they don't block each others' way after the serve. Again, they must try so the server gets into a good starting position for his second stroke.

Occasionally, you see an offensive-defensive combination. Your Austrian team colleagues Chen Weixing and Robert Gardos play together. What is important here?

The active player should be able to react very well to offensive balls, which means that he should be able to block well and counter loop well. The consistency of the defensive player should be above average when attacking.

The service choices are reduced because of the limited placement possibilities. There are fewer aces in doubles than in singles. Still, the service is very important for the opening of the game. What is the difference between serving in doubles and serving in singles?

Because of the reduction in placement, the quality must be above average.

How many different varieties do you signal to your partner with your fingers under the table?

Six.

What are the most tactical placements that can be used in the doubles in general?

Against a left-right combination, in the middle of the table; against two right-handed players, move to the according backhand side.

What kind of social behavior is absolutely necessary for a good doubles pair?

They must be willing to compromise.

What is the worst mistake a partner can make?

Stubbornly play his singles tactics.

Are you talking to your partner during the set when things don't go well? What is important then?

If necessary, you should also talk during the set about tactics and adjust the tactics accordingly.

Some experts maintain that in view of the speed of the game, doubles today are more difficult to play than singles. Others say that you can't compare this, singles and doubles are two completely different games. What do you think?

I think that doubles are physically less demanding than singles. Therefore, the mental (tactical and emotional) demands are higher because of the compromises with your partner. Singles and doubles are different in their demands and can therefore only be compared roughly with each other.

Werner Schlager and Karl Jindrak became European Champions in Aarhus 2005

Doubles partners who played together for many years often became good friends. What about you and Karl?

Exactly. Despite, or perhaps because of, our partially very different personalities, we became very good friends.

Does the coach play a different role in singles than in doubles?

His role is not completely different from that in singles. But the coaching of more than one person is more complex, and it is more difficult to find winning tactics.

Some consider the future of the doubles in danger in the long run. The Olympic Games were the beginning because there was no extra doubles event. In tennis, it also started slowly. Today, there are separate doubles tournaments with specialists whom hardly anybody knows. How do you see the future of the doubles?

I don't see this danger. The doubles were included in the team event in Beijing. The doubles will not lose its right to exist. It looks different in the mixed doubles; this event is dying already.

To play doubles is *always a challenge for me.*
Doubles demand *the ability to compromise.*
The modern offensive doubles *has many fans.*
If you want to be successful in doubles,
you must invest many years.
If my partner makes a foul serve at 10:10 in the seventh set, *all hell is loose.*

⑧ FITNESS AND ATHLETICS

8.1 Endurance

"Every third session is fitness training."

Fitness and athleticism play an important role in modern table tennis. Twenty years Ago, training at the table was by far the main component of practicing. Now all the top international players are physically well trained although the men are generally better trained than the women. How much time of your training is taken up by physical training in general?

At the moment, two training sessions at the table are followed by one session of endurance or strength training; that means every third session takes place away from the table. Ten years ago, I played five times as many sessions at the table before I started with endurance or strength training.

The five elements of physical training are endurance, power, speed, flexibility (agility) and coordination. Let's take one at a time and start with endurance. A table tennis player doesn't need to run a marathon (which might even do more harm than good) but seriously, how do you go about training general endurance?

Generally, you should take a fitness test every six months to assess your individual aerobic and anaerobic threshold of your cardiovascular system. Only if you have this data can you work productively on your endurance. An absolute minimum for me is one training session a week with endurance exercises (bike or running) for at least 30 minutes near the anaerobic threshold (heart frequency that increases your cardiovascular fitness). In connection with daily table tennis training, it should be possible to keep a minimal basic endurance. If you want to increase your endurance level, increase the quantity and time of the weekly sessions. Endurance training should also be used to regenerate quicker. For that, you use aerobic exercises.

Conclusion:
a) season preparation:
   program to build endurance: four to five sessions a week plus
   regeneration if necessary

b) competition period:
   normal program: one or two sessions plus regeneration if necessary
c) relaxing or transition periods:
   maintaining your endurance: one session

At least what distance should a good table tennis player jog each week?

About ten kilometers is enough for me.

What do you think about swimming and cycling as endurance sports for table tennis players?

They are just as good as running and less demanding on the skeletal system.

Being Austrian, you must have a special connection to skiing. Alpine skiing is less suited for general endurance but surely good for strength, strength endurance and coordination. Cross country skiing is surely an intensive endurance sport. Did you ski?

I tried it as a child, but I was not too enthusiastic about it.

Do you like endurance training that follows the saying: "Jog to relax mentally and physically," or do you prefer to stand at the table?

I prefer standing at the table.

Apart from general endurance, there is specific endurance during the game at the table. How do you increase the endurance ability to train and play at a high level without getting into the anaerobic area, producing too much lactic acid and getting tired?

The specific endurance is what is left over if you take away the efficiency of my movements from my general endurance. This means that you can either improve the efficiency of your movements or your general endurance to play for a long time at a high level.

There are sports scientists who maintain that general endurance is a presupposition for achieving top performance. Do you agree with this hypothesis?

Absolutely.

In professional soccer, regenerating jogging at the end of a match or the next day is common practice. Table tennis is not soccer, but do you also do some regenerating exercises at the end of hard competitions?

I use regenerative endurance sessions when I need it.

Do you have an adviser or a special coach who plans your endurance program or are you a "self-made man?"

There has been a fitness coach (Claus Bader) available to me for many years. I learned a lot from him and am grateful for his cooperation and friendship, which has developed over the years.

What is your time for the distance of 5000m?

I will never voluntarily run that far. I prefer to cycle.

What is the farthest you have ever run?

About twelve kilometers.

Every sport makes specific demands on the players. Who needs more general endurance, a tennis or a table tennis player?

It must be a tennis player because he must run a lot more and longer.

Different coaches maintain that it is more meaningful to shorten the training sessions and increase the intensity and concentration but train more sessions. Instead of playing twice a day for two hours, practice three times a day for 80 minutes. Do you agree or do you have other proposals?

I agree entirely concerning the sessions at the table.

The whole playing rhythm has been changed by shortening the sets. The whole game has become more intense, more concentrated and psychologically harder. Does this also have effects on the planning of endurance training?

The game became more intense but also shorter. I think that the demands in competitions lowered due to the different way of scoring. The general tendency of table tennis to play faster all the time demands a continuous improvement of physique.

Let's assume a coach and his player are not particularly bothered about endurance training; what would you tell them?

I would tell them that I would have had fewer injuries if I had recognized the importance of fitness earlier.

Keyword: doping. Especially in endurance sports, there have recently been some spectacular doping incidents. In cycling, EPO became well known because it increases endurance performance. Sadly, there were also cases in soccer and tennis. Could EPO also play an important role during hard training periods or intensive competition periods?

Surely one of the many necessary factors in top sports could be influenced positively. But what price do you pay? The one who uses doping in table tennis is really very stupid! It is possible to get right to the top without any doping.

General fitness is defined by sports science as the ability to overcome fatigue. Every athlete at the top level is interested in this. Apart from training, doping is a possibility to increase this ability. Is table tennis really as clean as everybody maintains?

The physical components are not quite as important in table tennis in comparison to other sports. General endurance, which can easily be gained without doping, is enough to make it right to the top in table tennis. Therefore, I can't imagine that somebody is so stupid to use doping to increase his endurance to unnecessary heights. That doesn't make any sense – at least not to me.

If you run a marathon, *you must be crazy.*
Endurance training *can't be fun.*
Jogging/Running is *sometimes relaxing.*
When I see running shoes, *I think of the feeling after running.*
If you don't train endurance, *you haven't understood anything.*

8.2   Strength

"The physical condition – and with it the training of strength – becomes more and more important."

If a table tennis player does not do general functional strength training, he will risk injuries. Playing table tennis means using the body in a very one-sided manner. This may cause problems with the muscles and complicated, long-term injuries.

Didn't you say yourself if you had trained your whole body better that some injuries could have been prevented? Can you briefly outline your history of injuries and tell us the reasons why they happened?

Apart from smaller injuries with my shoulders, hips and wrists, my back, knee and toe injuries were the biggest problems in my sporting career. I even had to undergo surgery on my toe. If I had trained my whole body more when I was younger, I would not have had so much pain and could have avoided the setbacks.

How important is strength training? What kind of strength training do you do? How much time do you spend on strength training?

Table tennis is changing constantly. The physical condition and strength training become more and more important. At the moment, I am doing strength training on average twice a week with the main emphasis on the upper body. I like strength training without weights. That means that I can also do my sessions while I am traveling, and I don't need a fitness studio.

For which parts of your body is strength training most important?

I think that, because of the frequent sudden arm movements, it is especially important to take care of the stability of the spinal cord. Therefore, I think an additional training for the non-playing side is absolutely necessary. Obviously, strong and speedy legs are also important. Unspecific strength training for the playing arm is, from my point of view, counterproductive because the fine control of the ball is influenced negatively.

Do you do push-ups and how many proper ones can you do?

I don't like push-ups. They strengthen the muscles of the arm too generally and reduce your control of the ball.

Is strength training for you mainly to prevent injuries or do you also notice a difference in your game if you practice the right amount?

That depends solely on the quantity of strength training. If you increase the quantity and the intensity, you will soon notice changes in your game.

At what age should a top sport-orientated youngster start with strength training?

As soon as you start playing regularly every day for hours, you should also do some other training for compensation.

Are there some strength exercises that you personally like best and some you don't like at all?

Naturally, I have my favorite exercises. I like working out my back and upper body muscles, and I am not so keen on upper leg and stomach exercises.

If I enter a fitness studio, *I took the wrong door.*
Strength training is *sometimes fun and sometimes torture.*
The one who doesn't do strength training *ruins his body.*
Strength training is *probably not so important*
for top sport-orientated amateurs.
Nothing works without strength.

8.3   Power and strength endurance

"Fast, strong legs are the basis for top athletes."

Power and strength endurance are important components to execute certain stroke techniques, like the topspin and the smash. But also the specific footwork for table tennis relies on these qualities. In modern table tennis, power and strength endurance are very important factors.

The topspin and the smash (both played with forehand and backhand) are very demanding for arm, shoulder and back muscles. The maximum acceleration needs a lot of power. Are you training these muscles especially to improve power? If yes, how?

No, I am not a fan of training with weights to improve the strength of my playing arm. The strengthening of these muscles should happen through very intensive table tennis exercises. Many balls practice is best suited to achieve this.

In tennis, the term "swing" is important for the execution of attacking strokes. The more a player is swinging his arm the less strength is needed. Is this applicable for table tennis too? What is your evaluation?

It is similar in table tennis. Swinging the arm means saving energy. If I can redirect this swing to the next stroke, I will be able to save energy. Learning this efficiency is one of the basics of the modern table tennis game. I can still see room for improvement in this area, especially my forehand.

Personally, I think Jan-Ove Waldner is one of the players with the best swinging movements. I would also put Vladimir Samsonov in this category, whereas players like Wang Liqin or Ma Lin are using more strength. Which of the top players would you see more as a swing or strength player, or do you differentiate in a different manner?

That is a correct analysis. If table tennis looks "easy," the player is playing efficiently. Those who look as if they are working hard are wasting energy.

Table tennis demands extreme application of the body: Timo Boll with a forehand topspin

You also need power in your legs, starting with your feet. Explosiveness during sidesteps and shifting weight demands a lot of power. What exercises do you practice to improve your footwork?

All exercises where you have to turn a lot. Coordination should not be neglected either.

What do you think about jumping rope? Boxers, who use similar "dancing" footwork, like table tennis players, consider this very important.

Personally I don't jump rope. I don't think that it is harmful but specifictraining at the table is preferable to jumping rope.

Strength endurance is also very important, especially when playing against defenders. I can remember when I was only an amateur in the 3rd division that my arm became heavier and heavier with each loop. A professional should normally not have any problems with that. Did it happen to you? Thinking about your fi-

nal against Joo Se Hyuk 2003 in Paris, I think you went right up to your physical limits especially in the previous matches, which were extremely hard.

Yes, at the World Championships in Paris, I didn't have any strength left in the final. Up to now, my strength has always been sufficient.

How are you training muscular endurance most intensively? Do you do special training with many balls or is the normally high quantity of practicing sufficient for enough endurance?

Good basic endurance in combination with many balls practice should be sufficient.

Do you often have stiff muscles after hard matches or practice sessions?

Of course. For years, I have been using a very effective remedy against stiff muscles, which really causes small miracles (own experience)! If you are interested, you can get information at www.panaceo.com. After hard sessions, I always use PANACEO-Sport. My physiotherapist has less work then.

If you look at the top stars today, they all look very athletic with strong leg muscles, broad shoulders and a flat stomach. Twenty years ago, it was not like that. Is this the result of targeted muscular training and the knowledge that a well-trained body is more resistant and less prone to injuries?

Both. The development in table tennis in the direction of speed leads automatically to higher physical demands. Naturally, a well-trained body is less prone to injuries.

It is essential to use swing.
I regularly train power.
Powerful legs are the basis for a top athlete.
You need a lot of endurance against defenders.
I do get stiff muscles

8.4 Coordination

"When you serve, all the different movements must be coordinated perfectly."

The coordination of movement is the targeted steering of movements. We differentiate between rough, precise and very precise coordination. The earlier children have the possibility of collecting different experiences of movement, the better they can learn new movements. So it is important to aim for a broad basic physical education at an early age. Especially in table tennis, the demands of coordination on a player are very high because the game is extremely fast and the player must react within seconds to direct his movements. The stars of modern top table tennis show rallies with artistic stroke and running movements, which produce almost unbelievable images for the spectators. It is all a question of coordination.

Were you one of the best in your P.E. lessons at school? Which activities did you like, and which activities were not exactly your favorites?

I always liked P.E. After primary school, I went to a sports school where we had a lot of P.E., of course. The main sports at school were soccer, orienteering and climbing, which only partially satisfied my need for activity. Therefore, I really enjoyed the daily table tennis sessions. Each activity involving coordination was worth a try. Orienteering wasn't really my kettle of fish.

Which activities do you think are good in combination with table tennis? Which ones do you do?

I doubt that there are other sports that go particularly well with table tennis. It all depends on your personal preferences as to which sport you choose for compensation. Personally, I don't do any other sports for compensation. Of course, I go running regularly and do other compensating strength exercises.

Sport scientists maintain that children with good coordination are better suited for top sports later on. Therefore, it is very important to promote a lot of different activities during early and late childhood. Did you do this sort of training when you were younger? What is your opinion about this?

I never did training like that. Naturally, a broad physical education is an Advantage, but from my point of view, not a condition. Children are by nature always looking for new incentives. Top sports might therefore lose their attraction very quickly with children. Interesting and differentiated training for one sporting activity is probably the best.

If you have a child who is interested in sports, when would you start to practice specific techniques? When did your father start with you?

As soon as a child shows interest. I started to be interested when I was six years old. My father noticed my interest and took me to the training sessions. If a child doesn't show this particular interest, you should accept it.

Table tennis is a sport with high demands on coordination. Situations have to be guessed and anticipated in a split second. They have to be recognized, analyzed and then transformed into appropriate answers (movements). Naturally, players develop more and more automatic reactions and reflexes because of their growing game and practicing experience, otherwise a game on a fast level would not be possible. Still there are always new and difficult situations that demand decisions. What is particularly difficult in table tennis concerning this coordination?

The most difficult area is to find your own balance, the balance between automatic reactions and control. This balance also decides whether I am in top or poor form. You are always looking for the important optimal relationship between conscious and unconscious actions. If there is too much unconscious action, consistency and tactical decisions suffer. Too many conscious actions slow down the flow of the game and the quality of the played ball is poorer.

Some coaches say that a really top class player differs from a good player because his anticipation is better. Do you agree?

Vladimir Samsonov, a champion of anticipation, who can hardly be caught on the wrong foot

Partially. No doubt that good anticipation makes it easier to become a top player. But you can compensate poor anticipation with a lot of effort and physical fitness. The best example for that is surely Wang Liqin.

How do you judge your own anticipation?

No idea. Others may judge that. I am satisfied with my own anticipation.

Which player is excellent concerning anticipation from your point of view?

For me, the champion of anticipation is Vladimir Samsonov. You never get the feeling that you might catch him off-guard.

Can you improve anticipation through particular exercises?

Every irregular exercise improves anticipation.

Can you improve your reflexes with particular drills? Do you know some exercises?

I don't know if you can train your reflexes. What you can practice is your attention (ability to concentrate) and your eye-hand coordination. There are many well-known exercises for that.

Concerning the aspect of coordination, the service is the only movement that can be executed without the influence of an opponent. The player doesn't need to react to the opponent's return but can concentrate completely on the movement of the service. The service can be easily improved if the player has been coached well. Why is the service only trained so intensely at the top level and often completely neglected with amateurs?

During the service, different movements must be coordinated perfectly. Precise throwing up of the ball is just as important for the quality of the service as the movement of the hand or the twist of the body. There are no limits to creativity. It is a natural phenomenon to spend more time with those things that demand more progress at little expense. Therefore, you learn the less complex movements like the standard techniques and a simple serve first. Later on, you progress slowly and you invest more hours in finer details. The service training is part of that, a prime example for optimizing movements.

Do you know some special coordination exercises that improve the coordination of the playing arm (upper arm-forearm-hand)? For example: a player knows very well that he must close the bat more when blocking the ball but his playing arm does not perform this task. A player knows very well that the coming ball has a lot of backspin but the topspin movement is too slow or too flat.

Often there is a mistake within the self-perception of the player. He thinks that he has already opened or closed his bat far enough. In reality, he has only come halfway of the possible movement. Only the learning of self-perception leads to the top.

Some coaches make their players play with their weaker arm so that a left-handed player plays with his right arm. What do you think about that?

I don't think that makes a lot of sense. Obviously, it is a much favored way of increasing motivation. It is fun to compete this way. Whether this automatically results in an improvement of coordination in the stronger arm as a consequence is doubtful. Only very intensive training of the weaker arm would improve the self-perception so much that the stronger side would profit. From my point of view, that is a waste of time.

Can you explain why the number of left-hand players is increasing above proportion the higher the playing level?

According to the current world ranking list, there are about ten left-handed players among the top 50. I don't think that is a higher proportion.

Thinking about tennis, do you think it is advisable to play tennis and table tennis simultaneously at a certain age? Does the tennis game influence the table tennis technique?

In my own experience, playing tennis and table tennis at the same time is not advisable. The necessary finer movements in table tennis are negatively influenced.

Do you like playing tennis every now and again?

Rarely. My parents have been regularly playing tennis for many years, including tou naments. Sometimes my father is asks me for a match. Up to now, he hasn't beaten me yet. The last match was a few years ago though. He is getting better every year so the next match could be interesting.

Imagine that you had invited 10 children (absolute new beginners) for a trial for 30 minutes. What would you do in these 30 minutes to find out if they were talented to play table tennis?

I can see within a few minutes if they have control over the ball or not. You don't need any special exercises for that. It is enough if they just play table tennis with each other. The control of the ball is only one of many factors. But it is also possible to see their intensity, creativity and ability to concentrate.

If I hit the ball with the edge of the bat,
I should work harder on my coordination.
Without coordination, *you can't move for many balls.*
Coordination for me is *like daily bread.*
If I react with my reflexes, *I am often surprised by the result myself.*
It is possible *to train* the ability to anticipate.

⑨ PSYCHOLOGY

Every sporting action is influenced by emotional, motivational, intellectual and cognitive factors from a sport psychological viewpoint. The emotions of a player decide the observation and action of a player. Positive or afraid, both conditions will lead the player to different actions. The same applies for motivation. He will have difficulties to win if he is over or under motivated. It is not easy to transfer optimal motivation to optimal performance. Tactical thinking and acting before and during the competition are decided by the cognitive and intellectual abilities of a player. One of the guaranties for success is always keeping control of the game. Already these few examples hint at the large influence of psychology, which is one of the deciding components of achievement. It can't be expressed in percentages how large the role of psychology in table tennis is, but the following example should stress why the mind is the deciding factor in table tennis. A player is technically good, also tactically well educated, his physical condition is brilliant but in important competitions, which should bring him further up (independent of the level), he loses regularly. Fear of failure, aiming too high, pressure from the coach and many other factors lead to the fact that the players can't achieve the same performance in a competition that he did in training. Thus, they are the famous "training world champions." Then there are other players who, especially in tight situations, defend match balls without fear and full of confidence, and also turn around lost matches.

9.1   Mental Strength, Psychological Pressure, Nervousness and Fear, Rage and Frustration, Mental Training, Prestart Condition

"Before each of my matches, I have butterflies in my stomach."

If two equally strong players meet each other, it is often said that the head decides the game. How do you evaluate this statement and what is the meaning of "head?"

The strength of a player is defined by several components. One of these is mental strength because a mentally strong player is able to win matches despite physical deficits.

Let's look at the last European Championships in St. Petersburg. You beat Timo Boll in the team event against Germany. A few days later, you lost to him in the semifinals in the singles. Is that a question of the "head" or does it have something to do with tactical changes because you both know each other very well from many competitions?

In the team event, I surprised him with a new tactic (also a "head" thing). In the next game, he had the suitable answers. This is a good example of how close the players are at top level.

There are players who are regarded as being mentally very strong and others who are weaker. Is that the difference between a top 10, 50 or 100 player?

That could be the difference. As I said, mental strength is only one aspect of the total strength.

Where would you put Ma Lin, Wang Hao and Wang Liqin in terms of mental aspects?

Not very far away from each other. Wang Hao and Wang Liqin are usually on a very high level, Ma Lin is slightly below them.

Who are, from your point of view, mentally the strongest Europeans?

Samsonov and Boll.

How do you estimate yourself from the mental point of view? You are an experienced player and used to playing under pressure, but are there still situations for you that are psychologically demanding?

I am quite satisfied with my mental abilities. The experience of 30 years in table tennis does help of course. Still, I am constantly working to improve.

Did you have a really bad series in your career where you couldn't win important matches because of a psychological barrier? If yes, how did you manage to overcome this?

Naturally, I had mentally weaker periods. I never had a so-called bad series though. I had the biggest problems during my cadet and junior years. When you become older, you normally also become more easy going, mentally.

Table tennis is extremely fast. Every point is like a penalty: it's either in or out. How do you deal with losing easy points or missing a penalty?

The best solution would be not to think too much about one's hits, especially not the bad ones. You should always focus as quickly as possible on the next rally. That means a short technical analysis and then full concentration.

Also mentally very strong: China's aces, here World Champion Wang Hao

In many matches, players have good and bad phases. It seems important to channel your frustration because otherwise you become furious or adapt other behavioral patterns, which disturb your concentration. This is very obvious in the lower leagues. How do you deal with frustration?

You shouldn't allow yourself to become frustrated. If frustration is there, it is very difficult to get rid of it again. A mental coach knows some useful mechanisms of how to help you. I got some help.

So, you got professional help from a sports psychologist, for example, in mental training? Could this approach help some players gain more self-confidence and calm down during the match?

Yes, I did use help. I can only advise the help of a mental coach. Actors talk about stage fright even after 50 years. That is part of it, otherwise something is not right.

What about your nervousness before a match? How do you achieve an optimal pre-start attitude and what does it look like?

I agree that a certain basic nervousness is part of the game. I have butterflies in my stomach before every match. I think it helps to focus.

Some players are extremely nervous before a match or they get stiff in their arm when the score is close. Did you experience something like that and how did you get rid of it?

Nobody escapes getting stiff in the arm. A mental coach has got the suitable solution for this, but there is no general recipe.

World Champion! Werner has just played the deciding match ball in the final. He drops the bat, he can't believe it and then he cheers. An unbelievable tension is resolved.

If it is 10:10 in the 7th set, *it is 5:5 in my head.*
If I am down 0:4, *nothing is decided.*
If my opponent claims an edge although it wasn't, *I smile about it.*
If I am nervous before a match, *everything is okay.*
If I miss a serve at 9:9 in the 7th set, *I keep playing fully concentrated.*
If I am 3:0 ahead in sets and my opponent equalizes to 3:3,
an exciting 7th set lies ahead

9.2   Concentration, Trance, Psychological Tricks, Will Power, Body Language, Time-Out, Relaxation

"Watch the fist to measure emotions."

An exceptional player differs from an average player because of special abilities. The ability to concentrate plays an important role in this. How important is total concentration for you and how do you achieve that before a game?

A condition of total concentration is an optimal condition that I don't always achieve. In such a phase, I don't feel as much as an person in action but more like an observer and am happy about my moves.

Sometimes you watch games and think that somebody is playing as if being in the zone. Everything works without thinking and effort. Are you familiar with this condition and have you experienced it?

That is the optimal condition, and I manage to achieve that more and more often.

You read all the time that you have lost already if, during a match, you start thinking about the score (for example, it's 8:4 – now I only need three points... if I lose this set I don't have a chance any more... and so on). What do you think about in a game – only about the next point or also farther ahead?

Optimally, I think only about the "here and now." It is true that

Werner apologizes for a net or an edge. Fairness is a top priority.

thinking about the past and the future is only of little help.

Table tennis at the top level is known to be very fair. That sometimes looks completely different in the lower classes where you can find some sort of a psychological war where you try to put off the opponent all the time. What psychological tricks do you consider as being unfair?

I have learned not to judge psychological tricks. I just don't take any notice of methods like that.

The famous "fist" as an expression of will power and strength is generally common. You use it as well, but only in special situations. When do you use it, what do you achieve with it

Werner encourages himself with his fist, but only in important game situations.

and when do you think it is unfair from the opponent?

For me, it is a measurement of emotions. I don't consider it unfair if my opponent uses it.

Are you looking your opponent into the eyes or are you looking for eye contact to show him who is in charge?

I don't make eye contact very often; only when I want to evaluate his emotional condition.

You are born to be a champion. As the World Champion of 2003, you also belong to this group. What is special about a champion from a psychological point of view?

You become a champion through hard work. Mental strength must also be trained. Talent alone hasn't been enough for a long time to get right to the top.

Body language (mimicry, gestures and posture) tells you a lot about personality and current psychological state. Can you tell when you opponent is afraid or sure of victory?

Normally, yes. But there are some players who don't give away much about their psychological condition. Then it is difficult to evaluate.

How do you look at your own body language? You are known to be very quiet, withdrawn and analytical. Sorry, but I once called you the table tennis playing chess player.

Depending on the form of the day, I am sometimes more and sometimes less satisfied with the control over my body language. Naturally, I am aiming for total control during the course of a tournament. I am working on it.

During application training courses, the action of shaking hands is always pointed out. Do you draw any conclusions from the handshake of your opponent?

No. Conclusions about the psychological condition are only momentarily and don't apply for a long period of time.

The 1 minute "time out" has different meanings from a psychological point of view. Sometimes the players themselves take it, but usually it is the coach. How do you deal with the time out?

I take a time out when I lose control completely. That happens very rarely. The observing coach reacts often much earlier because of his different view.

Sometimes I have seen you talking to yourself in-between rallies. How important is that to you and what are you saying

Werner corrects himself, takes the bat into the other hand and imitates the stroke.

Building up new concentration in between the rallies, when using the towel or drying the hand behind the net.

Talking to myself is very important. The result of the immediate analysis after a rally is put in mental or spoken orders. These orders cover all areas of the game. For example: "Place the first ball to the middle" or "Stay calm and focused."

Do you have special rituals before the game because you don't feel well otherwise?

No.

Quite a few top sportsmen are superstitious and perform certain rituals that an outsider can't understand. Do you have rituals like that?

No.

After long competitions, Europeans see relaxation of the body and brain as very important. The schedule for professionals in Europe is very tight so that optimal relaxation loses out. What about your relaxation?

Physical and mental relaxation are very important for the achievements of athletes. They should be trained individually. I only have some problems with physical relaxation because of my age.

From a psychological point of view, you must differentiate between the singles, the doubles and the team event. In the singles, you are on your own; in the doubles, you have a partner; and in the team, it is the whole team. When is the pressure highest: in the singles, the doubles or the team?

It is easiest in the singles because you alone have the responsibility for the result. In the doubles, your partner too is affected by your achievements. In the team event, the hope of the whole team rests on your shoulders.

There are typical singles, doubles and team players. Which category do you belong to?

None. I enjoy playing everything.

When I play for the team, *I feel the responsibility.*
Relaxation after the game is *very important to me.*
When I take a time out *it is "5 to 12."*
If my coach takes a time out, *he thinks that it is necessary.*
I don't like it when my opponent *hides away for me.*

10 TRAINING

"I plan my training together with my coach."

From a sports science perspective, training is a complex process of actions with the aim of influencing improvement in sports through concrete plans.

Who plans your training: you yourself or you together with your coach?

I plan my training together with my coach. Today it has become very difficult to plan your training optimally because of the many competition commitments. Let's take the year 2008 as an example: it started with the Europe-Top-12, followed directly by the team World Championships. In May, we won the Champions League. Then there were the Olympic Games and just afterward the World Cup followed by the European Championships. In-between these "highlights," I played several Pro Tour events and other tournaments.

When you are travelling, how often do you train and what kind of training are you doing?

Usually, I manage about ten sessions a week, six table tennis sessions, two endurance sessions and two strength training sessions.

Let's assume you had a home league match on a Sunday, the following weekend you play a Champions League Match in Granada for which you have to leave the Friday before. What would your training schedule look like from Monday to Friday?

A typical week could look like this:

Monday:	a running session for regeneration
Tuesday:	a table tennis session and a strength session
Wednesday:	a table tennis session
Thursday:	a table tennis session and endurance training
Friday:	a table tennis session

On some days during the preparation phase of the season, players practice two to three times a day. How many hours of table tennis practice are possible in one day?

I cannot practice table tennis more than three hours (two sessions) a day since the operation on my toes.

Short, but effective, was Kalin Kreanga's answer to the question of how long one training session should last. Is it true that today concentration and intensity are more important than long-lasting training sessions?

That depends. An experienced player like Kreanga knows exactly what he must practice. His concentration during training is optimal. Surely he trains less quantity in comparison to a less experienced player but his training quality compensates easily for that. The rule is: the more quality you have in training, the shorter the sessions can be.

How long is an optimal training session for you and what should it include?

My optimal training session consists of 15 minutes warm-up, 60 minutes table tennis and 15 minutes stretching.

How long do you warm up before a competition?

There is no golden rule for that. Sometimes you don't know the exact start of a match. Therefore, I always try to be in the hall two hours before the match starts so I can warm up under ideal competition conditions. During the 15-minute warm-up, I do some running and gymnastics. The same rule applies here: everybody should do their individual warm-up program. Individuality is the key.

I assume that every training session has a main focus. What main focus could that be?

Technique, service, footwork and so on.

Do you practice your services during each training session with many balls?

Normally I don't do any extra service practice because I include them in my exercises designed for competition. If I decide to practice them, I do them at the end.

Are there some days where you don't feel like practicing and you have to force yourself to go?

Yes, of course.

Do you play competition matches during training? Do you sometimes play for money, a meal or something like that? How important are training matches?

I often play matches during training but only for the honor. I consider training matches to be very important.

Critics of modern table tennis, among them quite a few coaches and players, maintain that it is almost impossible to train properly because of the number of tournaments (national leagues, champions league, national championships, continental championships, world championships, pro tour, Olympic Games and many more). The Chinese have much better opportunities to prepare intensively for important tournaments. What is your opinion about this?

I agree. The associations should not "overload" the list like this.

You are an experienced player and self-critical enough to tell what you did wrong during your training in the past. What did you change and do you think that completely new methods and ways of training could be developed?

In the past, the quality of my training wasn't good enough. New methods will be developed, of course. That is a normal continuous process as long as knowledge increases.

If you don't warm up, *you can't be saved!*
Meaningful training is *only possible with full concentration!*
Too much training is *as bad as too little!*
"A lot of training = good performance" is *not true!*
During good practicing session, *you are happy!*
After practicing is *more practicing!*

11

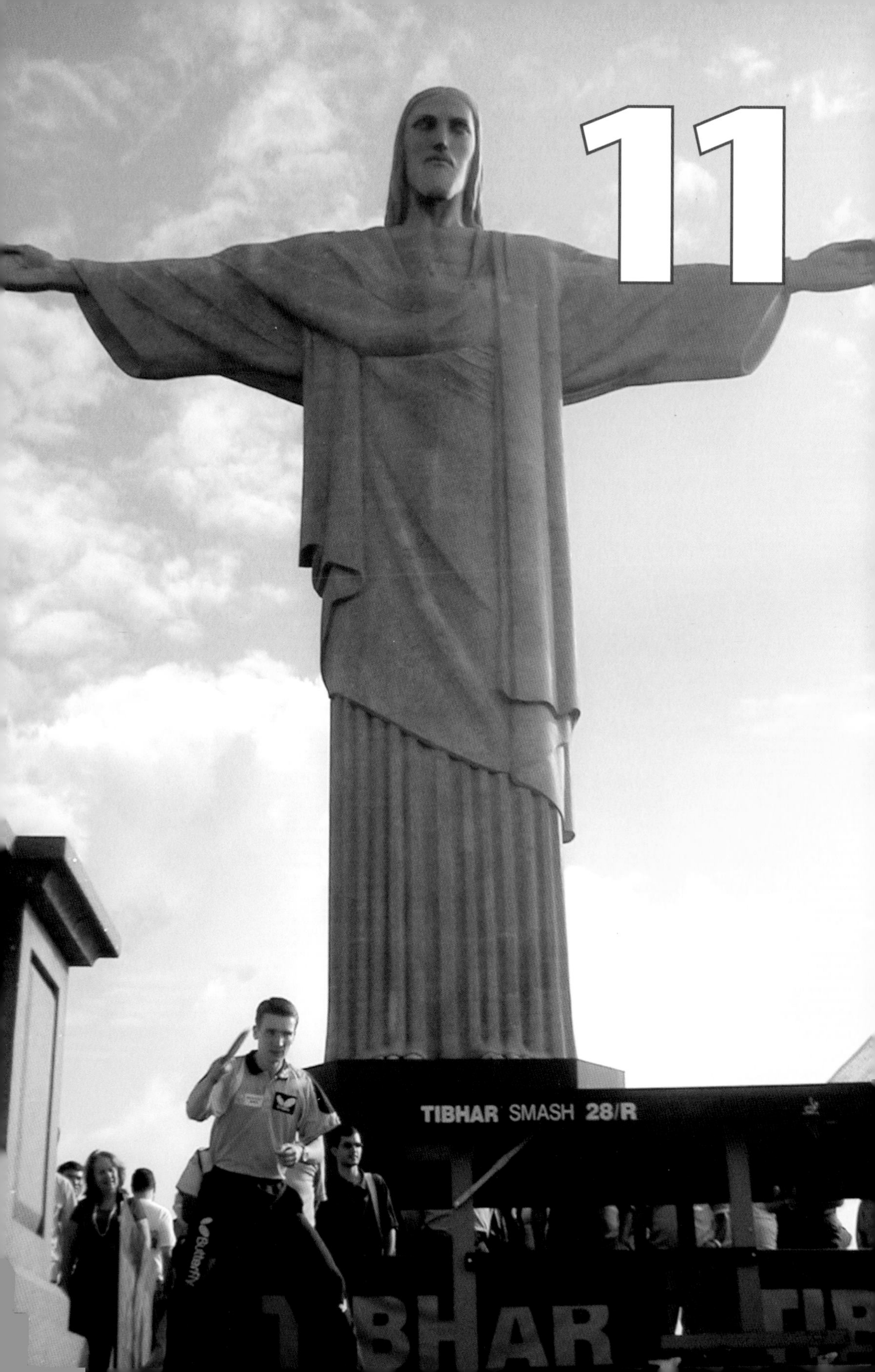

11 RESUME AND VISION

At the end of our interview series, we want to conclude with a review of our sport, show perspectives and have a good look at your big project, The Werner Schlager Academy. But one question first: „How did you feel about this series?"

This interview series helped me to understand this wonderful sport even better. We talked about many topics, which you as a sportsman probably don't think about so much.

Your life changed fundamentally a short while ago. At the beginning of February, you and your partner Bettina Mueller became the proud parents of your son Nick. How did you experience this event and how is it going to influence your life as a professional?

I am very grateful that I could experience the birth of my son. You see the real meaning of life just in front of your eyes. This intensive, positive time has influenced my private and professional life dramatically. Naturally, my professional engagement will be adapted to the needs of my son.

Could you imagine, that your son, if all the conditions are right, could also become a table tennis professional? Would you support that?

I would support that, of course. The genetic presuppositions are not bad but the most important thing is if he himself wants to play.

Apart from your private life, your business and table tennis life is also about to change quite a lot. The Werner Schlager Academy (WSA) is being built at the moment in Schwechat, a suburb of Vienna. The WSA will be, together with the German Table Tennis Center in Dusseldorf, the biggest table tennis center in Europe. When do you expect the official opening?

The building process will probably be finished in the summer of 2009.

How did you get this idea?

My friend and business partner Martin Soeroes asked the right questions at the right time.

Who will run the center? Who are the sponsors?

The "Werner Schlager Company GmbH," which is Martin Soeroes and me, will run the center. The most important sponsors at the moment are the town Schwechat, the region Niederosterreich and the country Austria. Naturally, we are also in contact with potential sponsors from business.

Whom is the WSA going to address?

The WSA is a center for table tennis competence, which will make offers to all age groups and levels of table tennis players.

How many boarding places do you have?

Werner is the last European World Champion since 1997, when the Swede Jan-Ove Waldner won the title before him.

There will be cooperation with a playgroup and schools but no classical boarding school.

Have you looked at possible coaches?

Of course. There will be international high class coaches. But at the Moment, I am not at liberty to quote names.

Did you pick Schwechat as a strategic place (South/Southeast Europe) on purpose?

The location of Schwechat came up automatically because of its excellent infrastructure and the proximity to the airport in Vienna.

What job are you going to take at the WSA after your active playing career? What are you doing now already?

163

I am responsible for all relevant decisions considering the sporting aspects of the WSA. I will also offer my experience to the group of coaches.

Finally let's talk about the present situation of our sport. What changed, positively or negatively, in the professional sport you have been part of during the last twenty years?

The whole development to a professional level in table tennis is surely positive. A mental and fitness coach are, for example, absolutely necessary in professional sports. Negatively are the constantly increasing numbers of competitions, especially for youngsters. In the general classes, you can still manage some kind of regular training. This has got to be reduced. The youngsters must have enough time to train properly.

What is missing in Europe that would make table tennis be recognized more as a professional sport?

We need more really good professional players, professional efforts and more presence of the media. The ITTF and ETTU really need to put some effort into this.

Why is the membership of amateurs stagnating or even decreasing in many European countries, including the strongest country, Germany?

I can't see a clear negative trend, but one thing is for certain: Europe needs the right impulses to bring table tennis forward again.

A word about your home country, Austria: What happened through your successes and those of the national team? Was there a boom?

Yes, the membership increased and is still increasing.

Where lies the future of table tennis? Do you really believe that table tennis may become a "big sport" like the ITTF President Adham Sharara always maintains?

Table tennis is already a big sport in some countries. To reach the world stage, all have to work with professionals, including the regions, clubs, coaches and active players.

One word about the game itself, how is table tennis going to develop in the future after there have been made so many changes so fast during the past years (the ball, scoring, the service and the glue ban)?

The ban of glue slowed the game down and made the rallies a lot more fun to watch. The change in scoring made the game more interesting. Further rule changes are not necessary.

How would you stop the to and fro about gluing, boosters and tuners so that finally things are clear again for players, coaches, umpires and spectators?

The ITTF should only come up with rules that can be controlled everywhere. Therefore, it is really necessary for them to take action.

Dreams and visions have often changed humanity and the world. Do you have a vision for table tennis?

More media attention through more professionalism.

In detail, how do you think that more attention of the media can be achieved?

On the one hand, more professionalism in sport leads to better results and that leads automatically to more media attention. On the other hand, you can improve a lot of things in the way you handle the media.

And now, the obligatory question: When does the World Champion quit playing? In September, you became 38 years old, an age where you might think of stopping.

I very rarely think about finishing. I am still enjoying table tennis a lot. I will probably start thinking seriously about stopping if my body forces me because of an injury.

Werner, it was not only a great pleasure talking to you but also an enrichment to conduct these interviews for the Butterfly News series. Good luck to you, your family and the WSA.

Thanks also to Butterfly for this opportunity, to the readers for their attention and to you for your cooperation! It was a pleasure.

Discovered the world through table tennis: Werner Schlager during a promotion in Rio de Janeiro.

12

Numbers, Dates and Palmarès

Name	Werner Schlager
Birthday	28. September 1972
Place of Birth	Wiener Neustadt
Club	SVS Niederösterreich
Sponsor	Tamasu Butterfly Europa

Career Highlights

1987 Junior-EC in Athens: Bronze with Karl Jindrak in the cadet doubles

1989 Junior-EC in Luxemburg: Bronze with Karl Jindrak in the Junior Doubles

1998 European Championships in Eindhoven: Bronze with Karl Jindrak in the Men's Doubles

1999 World Championships in Eindhoven: Bronze in the Men's Single

2000 European Championships in Bremen: Bronze in the Men's Doubles with Karl Jindrak

2002 European Championships in Zagreb: Bronze in the Men's Single, Bronze in the Mixed Doubles with Liu Jia, Bronze in the Team Event with Chen Weixing, Qian Qianli, Robert Gardos and Karl Jindrak

2003 European Championships in Courmayeur: Gold in the Mixed Doubles with Krisztina Toth (Hungary), Bronze in the Men's Doubles with Karl Jindrak

2003 World Championships in Paris: Gold in the Men's Singles

2005 European Championships in Aarhus: Gold in the Men's Doubles with Karl Jindrak, Silver in the Team Event Chen Weixing, Robert Gardos, Kostadin Lengerov, Karl Jindrak, Bronze in the Mixed Doubles with Liu Jia

2007 European Championships in Belgrad: Bronze in the Men's Doubles with Patrick Chila

2008 Europe Top-12 Victory in Frankfurt
European Champions League (2007/2008) Victory with SVS Niederösterreich
Fourth place in the Men's Team Event at the Olympic Games
European Championships in St. Petersburg: Bronze in the Singles, Silver in the Men's Doubles with Trinko Keen (NED), Bronze in the Team Event

2009 European Championships in Stuttgart: Silver in the Singles, Bronze in the Team Event

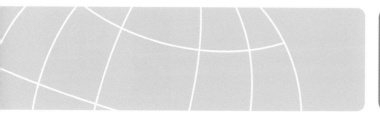

World cup
1999 Xiaolan (China): second place

Europe Top 12 Tournament
2000 Alassio: first place 2003 Saarbrücken: third place 2004 Frankfurt: second place 2006 Copenhagen: second place 2008 Frankfurt: first place

Participation in Olympic Games
1996 Atlanta – 2000 Sydney – 2004 Athens – 2008 Peking

PRO-TOUR
Werner Schlager is the only player in the world, who could qualify for all Final Tournaments of the best 16 players in the world since the PRO-TOUR was introduced in 1996. Also in the Doubles with Karl Jindrak (the only pair in the world) he reached the Final PRO-TOUR Tournament every year when it was played from 1996 to 2005.

Austrian Individual Titles
1995, 1996, 1997, 1998, 1999, 2000, 2001, 2002, 2003, 2004, 2005, 2006 Schlager became Austrian Champion in the Men's Single.

1990, 1991, 1992, 1995, 1996, 1998, 1999, 2001, 2003, 2004, 2005 Schlager (and Karl Jindrak) became Austrian Champion in the Men's Doubles, 2006 with Chen Weixing.

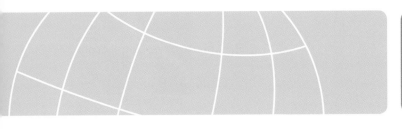

1994 (with Karin Albustin),1997 (Karin Albustin), 2001 (Judith Herczig), 2002 (Liu Jia), 2004 (Judith Herczig) Schlager won the Austrian Championships in the Mixed Doubles.

Werner Schlager (with SVS Niederoesterreich) was in the final of the European Champions League five times (2000, 2001, 2002, 2007 and 2008). 2008 SVS Niederoesterreich took the title home to Schwechat.

Werner-Schlager-Academy Betriebs GmbH, Moehringgasse 2-4, 2320 Schwechat, Austria, office@wsa-tt.com, www.wernerschlageracademy.com

Photo & Illustration Credits:

Cover photo:	Tamasu Butterfly Europa GmbH; © photo-dave/Fotolia.com
Photos:	Tamasu Butterfly Europa GmbH, Bernd-Ulrich Gross, Werner Schlager
Cover:	Sabine Groten, Aachen

LEARNING BALL GAMES

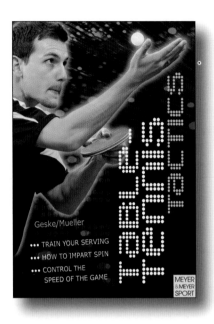

Geske/Mueller
TABLE TENNIS TACTICS
Your Path to Success

After a game, how often have you thought that you were the better player technically, but still managed to lose? In order to beat an opponent, you have to learn how to apply your technique correctly through a better tactical appreciation of each game as it progresses. This book will show you how.

120 p., full-color print, 50 photos, 36 illus., 1 chart
Paperback, 6 1/2" x 9 1/4"
ISBN: 9781841262994
$ 14.95 US/$ 22.95 AUS/£ 9.95 UK/€ 14.95

Barth/Boesing
LEARNING BASKETBALL

Especially written for kids, this book is easy to understand and offers a lot of fun while playing basketball. The little panther accompanies you throughout the book providing tips and explanations. Young players are given tips on fitness, technique, exercises and mistakes to avoid.

152 p., full-color print, 30 photos, 300 drawings
Paperback, 6 1/2" x 9 1/4"
ISBN: 9781841262505
$ 14.95 US/$ 22.95 AUS/£ 9.95 UK/€ 14.95

All books available as  E-books.

- secure & user-friendly

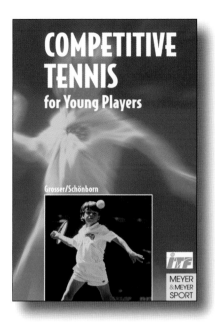
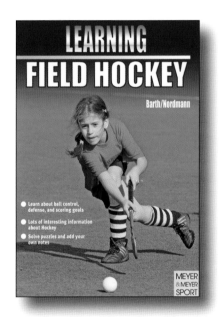